puppets
&masks

puppets & masks

ALBERT BOEKHOLT

Sterling Publishing Co., Inc.   New York

Translated and adapted by Louisa Bumagin Hellegers.

Photographs by Pierre Hériau, Daniel H. Feuillade, André Tahon Co., and Albert Boekholt. Drawings by Albert Boekholt, Olivier Desdoigts, and Marcel Temporal.

Text and drawings on pages 51-58 by M. Temporal.

28643

Library of Congress Cataloging in Publication Data

Boekholt, Albert.
    Puppets & masks.

    Translation of: Masques et marottes.
    Includes index.
    1. Masks. 2. Puppet making. I. Title.
II. Title: Puppets and masks.
TT898.B6313   1981   745.592'24   81-8572
ISBN 0-8069-7042-1   AACR2
ISBN 0-8069-7043-X (lib. bdg.)

Copyright © 1981 by Sterling Publishing Co., Inc.
Two Park Avenue, New York, New York 10016
Originally published in France under the
title "Masques et Marrottes"
Copyright © 1979 by Editions du Centurion
Distributed in Australia by Oak Tree Press Co., Ltd.
P.O. Box J34, Brickfield Hill, Sydney 2000, N.S.W.
Distributed in the United Kingdom by Blandford Press
Link House, West Street, Poole, Dorset BH1S 1LL, England
Distributed in Canada by Oak Tree Press Ltd.
% Canadian Manda Group, 215 Lakeshore Boulevard East
Toronto, Ontario M5A 3W9
Manufactured in the United States of America
All rights reserved

Contents

Fig. 1

Preface

This book does not pretend to cover the entire range of possible handicrafts related to the dramatic arts. Deliberately not touching upon the "acting" aspect of theatre at all, this book attempts instead to provide you with some of the techniques necessary for creating your own dramatic props and personalities—masks and puppets.

People sometimes minimíze the importance of a particular creative technique. Often this is because they do not realize that they can easily learn to do it themselves. This book intends to teach you various activities that are not only fun to do, but that will also help you to develop a creative imagination.

Through the years, masks and puppets have been made from almost anything—from carrots and pinecones to empty food containers or cartons. They have been sculpted from wood, stamped from leather, carved from stone in decorative murals, and made from thousands of other processes, some of which are considered to be classic.

The ideas in this book are limited to "proper" techniques that you can practice anywhere—at home, in a classroom, on a corner of a table—without a complicated setup or the mess of modelling, moulding or sculpting. Your workplace can be simply equipped and uncomplicated. With some paper, lightweight cardboard, felt, a little wood and only a few other materials, you can make some beautiful—and expert-looking—projects.

Another merit of the materials this book recommends is their rigidity. Paper and cardboard are flexible enough so that you can curve, roll or fold them at sharp angles, yet they do not have the elasticity of modelling clay. Amateur crafters sometimes tend to expect perfection from materials that are too malleable. In addition, beginners often strive only to make creations that are true-to-life (or caricaturelike) and which have no decorative appeal or artistic value. In making your creations, try to combat the influence of our photographic world, which discourages imagination. The difficulty of working with certain materials adds to this problem.

Another advantage of the methods discussed in this book for making masks and puppets is that they lead you away from traditional methods in which you work in two dimensions on flat surfaces, such as notebooks, chalkboards, canvas, etc. The exercises you find in this book are three-dimensional, and thus contribute to your developing a sense of size, shape and space.

The best masks are always those that differ the most from photographic representations or faces. The basic rule to follow in decorative mask-making is this: Try to produce a harmony of shapes and colors that expresses the spirit of the character you are creating; do not attempt to make a physical portrait or to fix one fleeting expression of a character. Dividing the construction into different levels—the eyes, nose, mouth—can help you to effectively combine all possible geometric shapes.

To construct a mask well, you must first have a precise idea of the character you are trying to permanently represent. Carnival masks, with horrible grins or unnatural grimaces, are not very useful in terms of good drama. They serve limited purposes, and you should avoid making them.

One last word of advice: Although some parts of your mask can remain white, you can generally enhance the effect you create by using color.

NOTE: A large number of the projects photographed in this book are not the work of the author. Often they are the work of beginners, which makes them more valuable as introductory aids.

MASKS

Designing a Head

Front view

It is well known that children depict only the expressive and movable parts of the face and do not usually consider the bulk of the skull. The result is a rather awkward-looking mask or puppet. It is actually quite simple to accurately portray the head. This can be done on a chalkboard in less than half an hour. Follow Figs. 2 and 3.

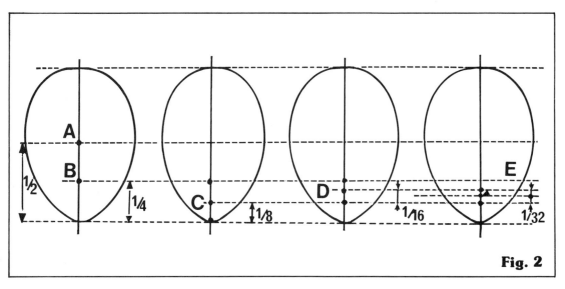

Fig. 2

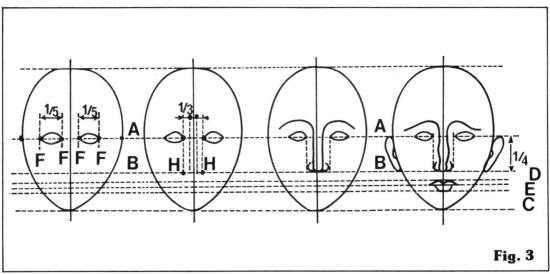

Fig. 3

1. Draw an egg and its vertical axis. Divide the egg in half heightwise (line A), and then in quarters (line B).

2. Delineate the bottom eighth (line C).

3. Locate one-sixteenth of the height by drawing line D between lines B and C.

4. Divide the distance between lines D and C in two equal parts (line E).

5. Return to line A and mark points F, which delineate five equal parts. You can immediately see how to place the eyes, which you situate in the middle of the total height.

6. Draw lines from the interior corners of the eyes to points H on line B. Then divide rectangle F-F-H-H vertically into three equal parts.

7. Notice that the bridge of the nose occupies the central third and that the nostrils are located on either side. The arches of the eyebrows prolong the nose round the eyes and can be of various shapes.

8. Place the ears between lines A and B. Draw the two lips between lines D and C. Note that the upper lip has two lobes and the lower lip has only one. Below the lips, the chin takes up one-eighth of the height of the head.

Clearly, by starting with the network of lines just described, you can create an infinite number of faces by adding only slight variations—for example, the hair, the arch of the eyebrows, or the nose or mouth. The proportions just given are easy to adapt.

Profile view

Begin again with the view of the face that you have just drawn. Next to it, draw a square of the same height. Divide the square into four horizontal quarters (see Fig. 4).

Draw the diagonal line A-B, which ends at the bottom towards the chin.

Next, just inside the square and symmetrical to the diagonal line, draw an oval curve. This should look like an egg whose thick end will be the skull and whose thin end will be the chin.

Erase part D-F of the curve (shown as a dotted line) and replace it with the nape of the neck D-E, with point E located one-quarter of the distance below the median M. Next draw curve E-F, which corresponds to the lower jawbone. Draw the ear

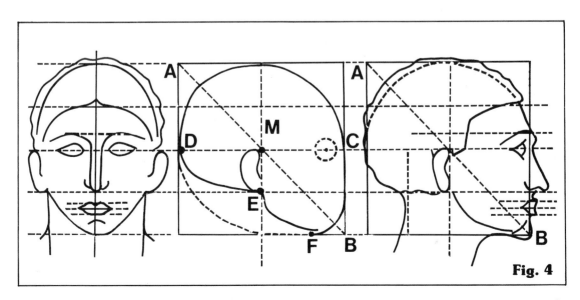

Fig. 4

between M and E (the second quarter in height).

Place a small circle on the horizontal median D-C to mark the location of the eye socket. On the final design, all that will be seen is the front part of this small circle, between the two eyelids.

Notice that the protruding portions of the eyebrows, nose, lips and chin are drawn outside, but just next to, the main square. Fig. 4 shows one way of drawing these features. Of course, you can vary the proportions in any number of ways: The nose can be long or short, hooked or turned up; the lips can be thin or fleshy, etc. Also draw the mass of hair just outside the basic oval curve of the head.

Now begin to draw the neck, which should be half as thick as the starting square. Many beginners are surprised to find that the face only occupies one-quarter of the square and that the head viewed in profile is clearly larger than the same head viewed from the front. These various facts cannot be overemphasized; they are important because they influence how you produce your masks and the heads of your puppets.

Take a disc made of wood or cardboard (Fig. 5). Notice that if you turn the disc slightly on its axis A-B, it takes the shape of an ellipse. The more you turn it, the flatter the ellipse becomes, but the ends of ellipse A-B do not become pointed. They never stop being curved, even when the ellipse is at the point when it could practically be confused with a straight line.

Now consider the vertical axis C-D. Remember that you are doing all of this to observe that an ellipse is merely a circle deformed by the perspective with which it is viewed (see Fig. 6).

Now take an example familiar to all schoolchildren: a globe of the world. Notice the equator, the large circles (meridians), the parallels of 45 degrees of northern and southern latitude and the two poles (Fig. 7).

Demonstrate what happens when the Earth turns round the axis of the poles: The meridian of point F, which was completely straight, becomes an ellipse. The large circle from point D also transforms into an ellipse. Now imagine that the Earth suddenly turns round an equatorial diameter. Point D does not move. It is point F that is displaced and the equator becomes an ellipse, just like the parallel circles at 45

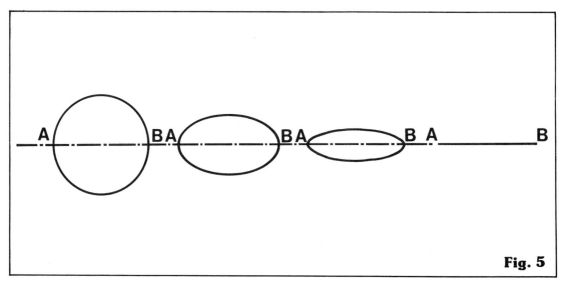

Fig. 5

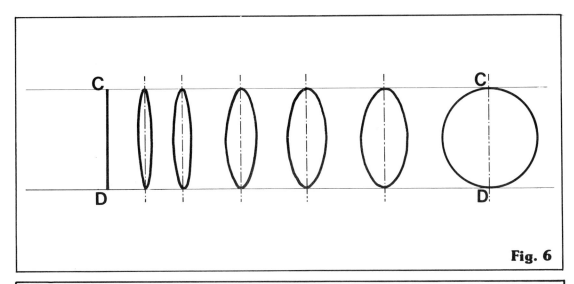

Fig. 6

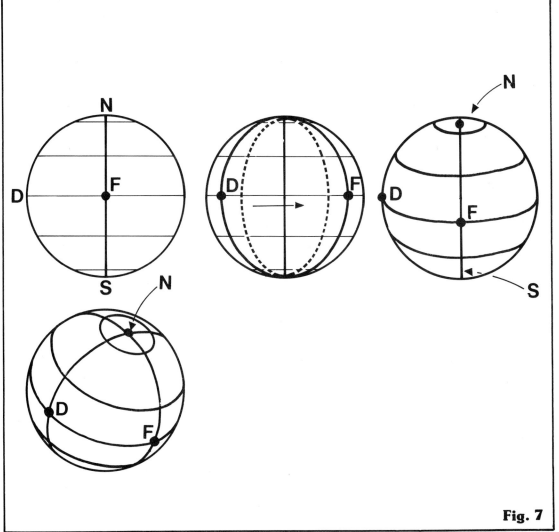

Fig. 7

degrees. Pole N passes in front; pole S passes behind and is invisible.

By combining the various movements just demonstrated, you can place points anywhere on the sphere, such that N-D-F will form a "curved-line triangle."

Look again at a head viewed from the front (Fig. 8). Compare the globe and the oval mass of the head. Draw circles on face F that pass through the eyes, the bottom of the nose and the hair. These circles seem to be straight lines.

If the head turns towards the left (G), the circles remain straight, but the "meridians" of the ears and the nose become ellipsoidal.

On the contrary, if the head bends towards the bottom (B), the line of the nose remains straight, but the horizontal circles become ellipses.

You can easily show that by drawing a sort of egg shape on whose surface you design differently inclined ellipses—for the nose, eyes, ears, etc.—it is relatively simple to draw a head in all possible positions.

Now draw some simple depictions of heads. Then correct these drawings according to the dimensions you have just learned. Such exercises can familiarize you with three-dimensional and spatial representation, and will thus help you to create correctly proportioned puppets and masks.

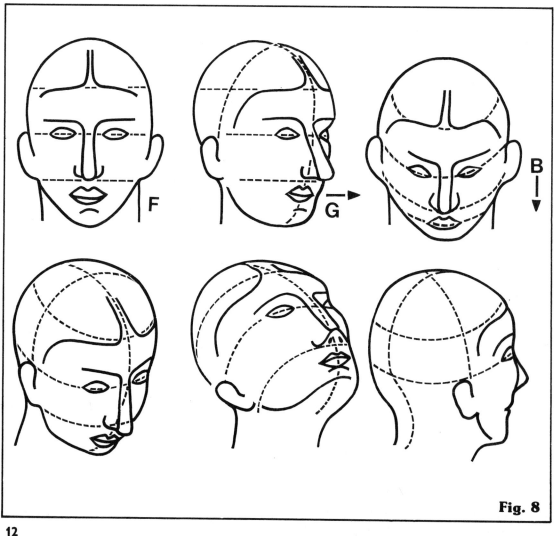

Fig. 8

A Game for Children:
Jigsaw Masks

Take a colorful piece of heavyweight cardboard. Cut out squares 8 × 8 inches (20 × 20 cm), on which you draw horizontal and vertical lines (see Figs. 9 and 10).

On each one of the resulting checkerboards, draw a different head. Make thick, clear lines, either with a soft-tip marking pen or with a paintbrush and dark ink.

Notice that the designs in Figs. 9 and 10 all have ten points in common with the lines of the internal squares. These are marked in the diagrams with thick black dots. It is important that you pass through each of these ten points in drawing your designs so that the faces line up.

Fig. 9

Fig. 10

After you have neatly drawn all of the faces, carefully cut along the vertical and horizontal lines. You should have a mixture of squares.

Mix up the pieces. Reorganize the squares to create funny faces—change the nose, eyes, mouth, etc., of the various original drawings. The new masks you create can be hilarious!

Another game you can play is to see if you and your friends can put together the original drawings without making any mistakes. Timing this attempt is a good way to test observational skills and your sense of logic.

Of course, you do not have to use faces like the ones suggested. When you design your own face, however, be sure that the connection points line up exactly.

Cardboard Masks

Creating a mask, a concrete representation of a character, starting with a picture of an abstract idea, constitutes one of the best exercises for learning stylization and decoration. Masks also make excellent wall ornaments, especially because of their relief.

Before you embark on a mask-making project inspired by the ideas in this book, you might consider studying some real masks. You can look at some photographs of existing wood or metal masks in books about native art, or you can visit special museums that specialize in colonial or native art.

When you begin to construct your own masks, first try to break up the model you are following into its basic elements. Cut the various pieces from thick cardboard, assemble them with glue in a collage-type manner and then paint the different parts. This is the technique that was used for the masks shown here.

Fig. 11

Fig. 12

Fig. 13

Flat Paper Masks

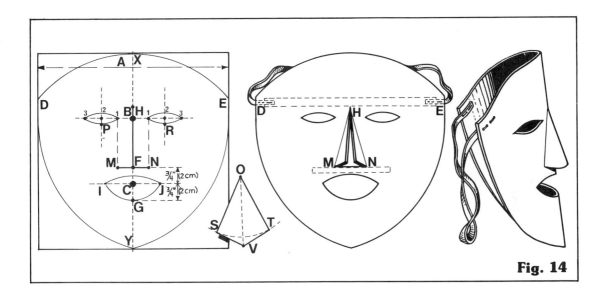

Fig. 14

This is the easiest procedure for making masks. It is especially appropriate for young beginners.

Materials

Heavy paper (Construction or drawing paper)

Pencil or crayons to draw on the paper you choose

Scissors

Strong glue

Flat, narrow elastic, preferably black or the color of your hair

Bright-colored water-base paints (you can use colored paper instead).

Drawing the mask

1. Use a piece of string to measure length A on your own face (see Fig. 14). Begin at your forehead and measure around your head, from one ear to the other.

2. Cut a square whose sides are as long as length A out of the paper you have chosen.

3. Draw the vertical axis X-Y of the square. Divide the square into three equal parts by marking points B and C.

4. Draw two horizontal lines, one each through points B and C. Line B marks the height of the eyes; line C marks the line of the closed mouth.

Eyes

1. Mark points 1, 2, and 3, spaced three-quarters of an inch (2 cm) from each other, to the right and left of point B.

2. Draw the vertical axes of the eyes through both points 2.

3. Using a 1½-inch (4-cm) radius, draw

Fig. 15

the arcs passing through points 1 and 3. Cut out the holes for the eyes along these arcs.

Mouth

1. Mark points F and G three-quarters of an inch (2 cm) from point C along the vertical axis.
2. Using F as the middle point and F-G for the radius, draw the lower curve of the mouth, I-G-J.
3. Draw the upper arc of the mouth so that it intersects line F-C in the middle.

Nose

1. Mark points M and N three-quarters of an inch (2 cm) to the left and right of F.
2. Mark H about three-eighths of an inch (1.5 cm) above B.
3. Slit lines H-F and M-N with a knife.

Perimeter

1. Using C as the central point, draw the arc D-X-E.
2. With the same radius, but using points P and R (on the edges of the eyes) as the central points, draw arcs D-Y and E-Y.
3. Cut out the mask following these three arcs.

Assembling the mask

1. Raise up the sides of the nose by folding along lines M-H and N-H.
2. Glue a strip of cloth or heavyweight paper to reinforce the narrow band that separates the nose and mouth (shown in Fig. 14 by a dotted line).
3. In the same way, reinforce the forehead, even with the spots where the elastic will pull when you wear the mask (also shown by dotted lines).
4. Attach the elastic. You can either sew it onto the mask, knot it or attach it with spread fasteners.
5. Now make the nose. With point O as the middle and using a radius equal to lines H-H or N-H, draw arc S-T (see drawing). Angle S-O-T can be larger than angle M-H-N. Cut out the quadrilateral S-O-T-V. Fold along O-V. The exact shape of the nose depends on how much separation you leave between S and T and on where you place point V on the mask. Glue this nose to the raised-up sides M and N on the mask. Decorate the mask with paint, if you wish.

The right-hand side of Fig. 14 shows the finished mask. Note that you can fold this mask completely flat along its vertical axis, so you can carry it easily in your jacket pocket!

Paper Masks in Relief

The procedure for making relief masks is very simple. Following Fig. 16, cut out an oval shape from a piece of thick paper, such as manila.

With scissors, split the paper egg to about mid-height, along line E-Y. Slide and glue the streaked part shown in the diagram under the opposite side, up to X'. This produces a sort of flattened conical relief. Reshape the curve of the chin after glueing.

The relief is the interesting part of this work. You can enhance the relief effect by creating shadows. In this way, you can also avoid having to color the facial features.

As you work on this mask, it is easy to add cheeks (or cheekbones) by attaching

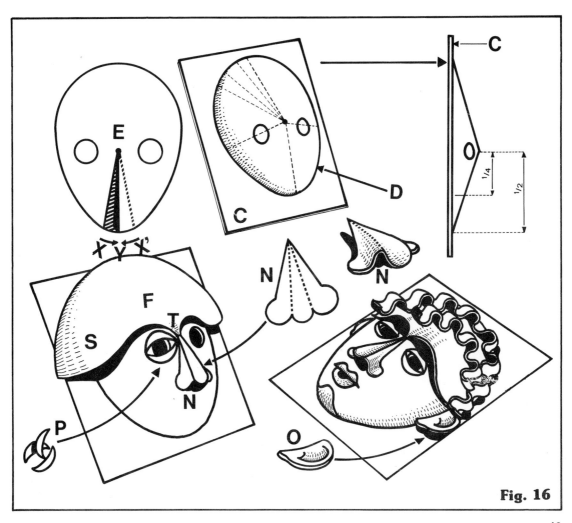

Fig. 16

an overlayer of cardboard to the face, connected to the chin. Glue the lips to this raised level.

Pierce two holes for the eyes at the mid-height of the oval, then smear the circumference D with glue and attach it to a piece of cardboard C. Be sure to use a glue that dries quickly and does not stain.

Cut out and fold some sort of nose shape from a piece of heavy paper. Glue the nose to the top quarter of the bottom half of the cardboard oval. Cut out a shape such as F in Fig. 16 from another piece of paper; this forms the arch of the eyebrows. Piece F must overlap the top of the oval, so that when you glue it on the face at T and then (after that has dried) at S-S (the streaked areas on the diagram), you produce a relief effect on the forehead.

If you want, you can begin this mask by glueing on the forehead relief. Consider various nose shapes until you discover one that is exactly what you want.

Cut out the appropriate shapes to form the eyelids P, lips and ears. To create the relief, glue only one edge of these parts to the base. The shapes you choose for these facial features give your mask your personal touch. Because the preliminary steps in mask-making are more or less the same for all the masks, changing these shapes enables you to use the same foundation to make many different relief masks.

All that remains is to decide what type of hair you would like to add to the mask. The hair can be more or less natural or totally decorative, depending on what type of hair you wish to add.

Creating one of these simple paper or relief masks helps you to prepare to construct a more complicated mask or a puppet. By learning about and experimenting with proportion, you can avoid making some of the errors common to beginning crafters—for example, placing the eyes so high that the face of the mask stares at the ceiling instead of the audience.

Twelve Decorative Masks

Simple masks made in the manner just described and then painted yellow or white can play a large number of dramatic roles well. If you add more design and a variety of colors, you can change the appearance even more. In fact, you will be surprised at how easily you can transform a simple creation by adding different designs and a variety of colors. Figs. 17 to 28 are some examples of what you can make:

Fig. 17 pictures a mask from British Columbia. The holes for the eyes are round instead of almond-shaped. Framing the eyes are a mask and some bright blue fish. The shapes on the forehead are dark brown. All the thin border lines are red.

The ancient Greeks were the inspiration for the mask in Fig. 18. The background is yellow or ivory. The nose is partly cut out and is only glued onto the forehead. The side plates are also only partly cut out and are glued only from the top, partially covering the mouth. Make the hair white or brown from yarn threaded through holes.

The mask shown in Fig. 19 is a Chinese design painted two colors. The background is rosy white; the design is black, as is the beard.

Fig. 20 also shows a Chinese mask. The background is royal blue; the large areas round the eyes are very dark brown and are decorated with pale yellow crescents. The rest of the mask is ochre and orange, the beard reddish orange.

The mask in Fig. 21 is Japanese. The background is ivory, the designs black and the mouth red.

The African mask shown in Fig. 22 is

Fig. 17

Fig. 20

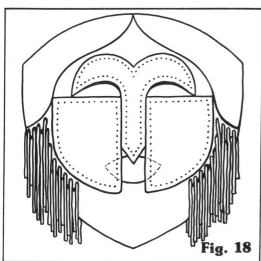

Fig. 18

Fig. 21

Fig. 19

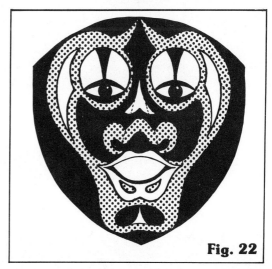

Fig. 22

Fig. 23

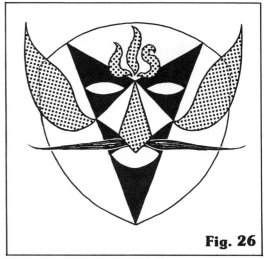

Fig. 26

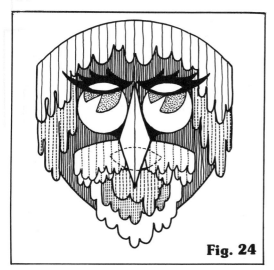

Fig. 24

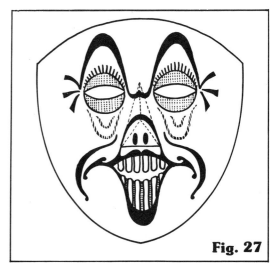

Fig. 27

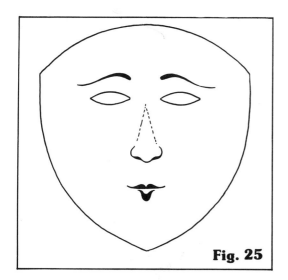

Fig. 25

Fig. 28

black and blood red and has pure white accent areas.

The remaining masks pictured are amusing: If you wear a mask like the one shown in Fig. 23, with a red background and brown designs, you will resemble a sinister pirate about to seize a ship; be sure to glue white cardboard teeth behind the mouth.

The mask in Fig. 24 could be Neptune, the sea god, or even a magician from the depths of the forest. The hair, mustache and beard are made of scallops of cutout paper, forming graded blue and green waves. The eyebrows are black (notice the holes for the eyes hidden in the black of the eyebrows). The nose is long and pointed.

Feminine characters are best portrayed with a mask like the one shown in Fig. 25, which is painted rosy white and tinged with blue around the eyes. The slight eyebrows are black; the mouth is tiny and is not cut out. Underline the base of the nose with an ochre or blackish-brown curve.

And here in Fig. 26 is the devil personified! Orange and red geometric shapes and a black mustache (made from waxed locks of hair held in place with a piece of wire) help create this striking mask. The ears are partly cut out and are glued to the base, which is made from gold- or copper-colored metallic paper. The flame on the forehead is cut out from the same material and glued in place.

If you wear the mask in Fig. 27, you will surely convince your audience that you are a jester or a clown. Do not forget to make the big white teeth and the pyramidal nose on which you glue a piece of cardboard, pierced to make nostrils.

On the other hand, the last mask (Fig. 28) will give you a learned and scholarly air. The background is deep pink, the glasses black, and the hair and eyebrows are strands of white yarn.

To complete this section, Fig. 29 contains several examples of noses you can use with any of the masks previously described. The nose on the far right is made of a lightweight rubber ball, which you slice in two places with a razor blade to create the opening pictured. Smear the cuts with a strong glue, and attach the nose to the paper mask. Let the glue dry well.

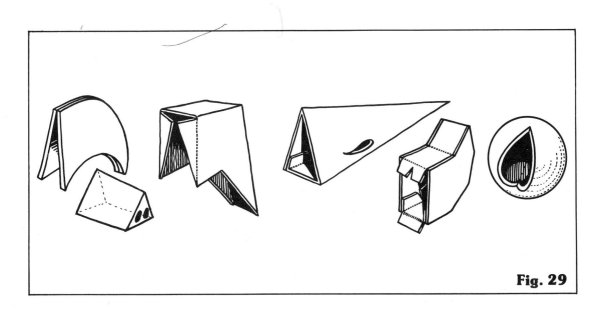

Fig. 29

Masks Constructed on a Stand

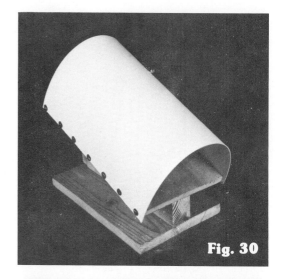

Fig. 30

This more complicated process requires that you construct a support stand, but it also increases the relief you can create.

Constructing the stand

1. Nail or screw a tilted shelf such as T in Fig. 32 to a pedestal such as P-S. The width of the shelf A should equal the width of your head. You can adjust the angle of the support any way you want—you might prefer a more vertical angle, for example.

2. Take a sheet of heavy cardboard about 10 × 14 inches (26 × 35 cm), curve it as shown in C in Fig. 32 and nail it to the support.

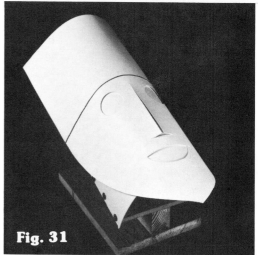

Fig. 31

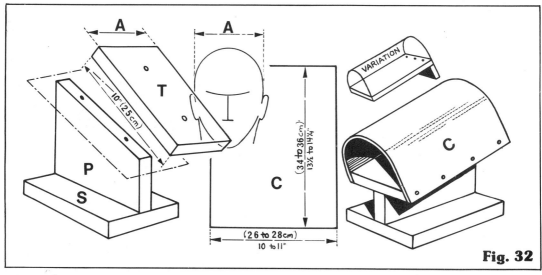

Fig. 32

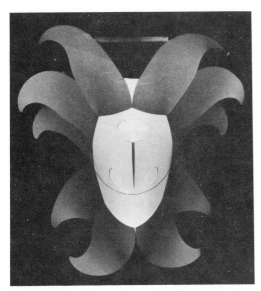

Fig. 33

c-d and at that point, draw line x-y parallel to a-b. Cut holes for the eyes along this line. Be sure to measure and mark the separation between your eyes before you cut, so you can be sure to see through the holes.

3. Indicate the placement of the nose by making two perpendicular slits at n.

4. Finally, cut out the mouth (unless your character is mute). You can shape the mouth in a variety of ways. Generally, try to make a big enough opening to allow the audience to clearly hear your voice from behind the mask.

Drawing the mask

1. With a piece of string, measure length l around your forehead from one ear to the other (Fig. 34).

2. Draw a line ab = l on a piece of heavy paper or lightweight cardboard. Then, using l as the radius and points a and b, respectively, as the midpoints, draw two arcs which intersect at c. Draw the axis of the mask, c-d. Measure one-fifth of line

Assembling the mask

Attach the framework of the mask to the stand you built, using a piece of string f (Fig. 34). Lift up the two flaps you cut at n, on to which you glue the nose. Notice that the height of the mask extends quite a bit above the eyes. You can cut out a more definitive shape later when you add decorative touches to the mask.

After you have completed the mask itself, attach a piece of elastic so it is level with the line of the eyes. Fig. 34 shows some ideas for adding more relief to your creation.

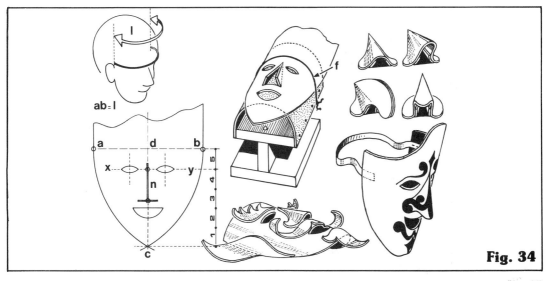

Fig. 34

Two Simple Masks
Formed on a Stand

You can make the two different cardboard masks described in this section according to the directions you just followed for constructing a mask on a stand.

Begin both masks by making a custom-fit paper pattern. Wrap a piece of paper

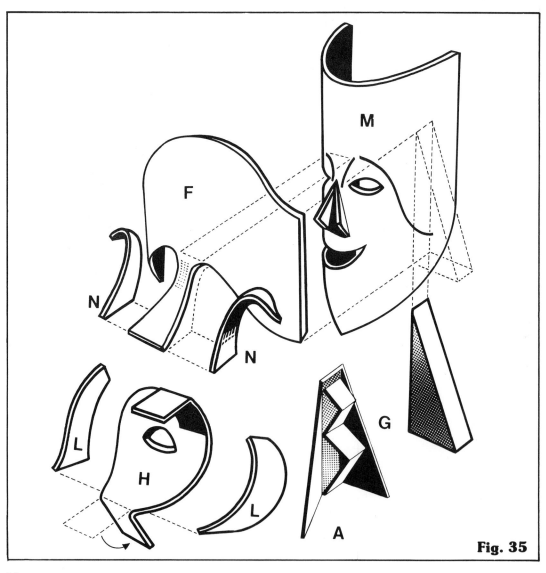

Fig. 35

around your face, from one ear to the other, and mark the location of the holes for the eyes, mouth and nose to correspond with your own.

Trace this pattern on to lightweight bristol board, strong construction paper or very thin cardboard. Cut out the pattern to look like piece M in Fig. 36. Attach this foundation piece to your stand with thumbtacks or several strips of gummed paper or adhesive tape.

Now draw the face for your mask. Break the design into the various parts that you plan to curve, fold and re-bend after cutting them out to produce the relief effect.

Glue these different pieces on to the background curve M, and also to one another. Use gummed strips of kraft paper to do this; these dry almost immediately so you can work quite quickly.

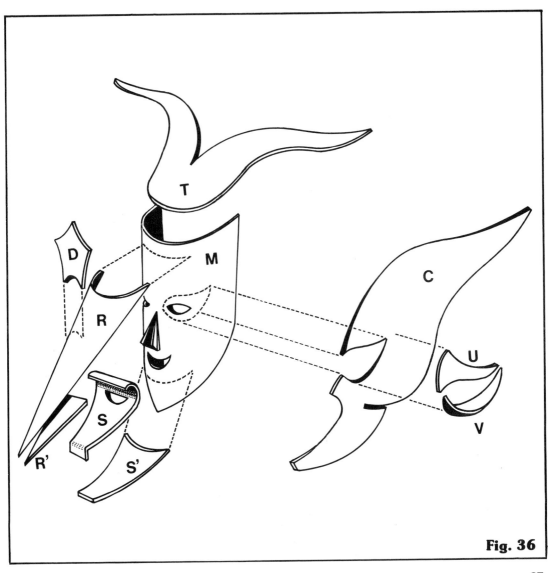

Fig. 36

Sorcerer's mask

The parts of this mask are shown in Fig. 35. To begin, glue pieces R and S onto the base M. Then glue on pieces R′ and S′.

Cut out side pieces C so that they fit to connect with the edges of R and S. Carefully mark the hollows that surround the front of the eyes.

Measure and cut out piece T to attach to the top of M and along the top edge of C. This piece determines the curvature of the horns.

Add pieces U and V round the eyes and piece D at the top of the nose.

In assembling these masks, you will probably notice that there are some holes in the construction that are difficult to conceal (for example, between D and R). To eliminate these spaces, you can stretch pieces of gummed tape across them to make the mask one solid mass.

Antique mask

To make the antique mask shown in Fig. 36, glue the left curved side of piece F on to the background M, so that you form a protruding forehead which connects to the hollows of the eye sockets.

Next attach piece H under the nose and to the bottom of M (whose point you cut to fit while you are joining the parts). Cut pieces L and N to fit and glue them in place as well. Finally, make the side pieces G separately and glue them in place. Note that you reinforce the G pieces with strip A, which is accordion-pleated.

Of course, you can change the arch of the eyebrows, the length of the nose or chin, and the shape of the ears (which you can also replace with horns). Your results will be an entirely different—and creative—project.

Obviously, this mask cannot be complete until you have colored it. You can use either water-base paints, a collage of colored papers, or even appliqués of felt which you glue on with a good fabric glue.

Importance of relief

Do not think that you are limited in your decorating plans by a curved surface. On the contrary, you should strive to create adjoining areas that contrast relief and shadows, as shown in Fig. 37.

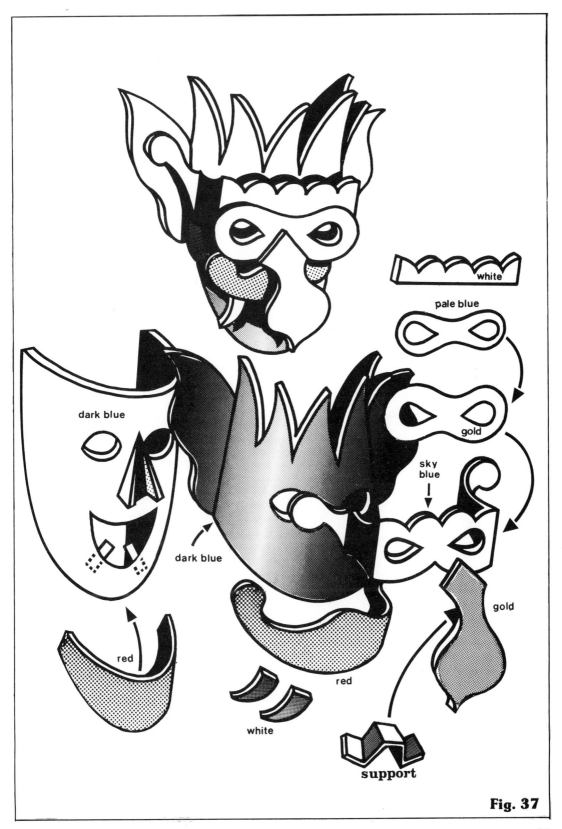

white

pale blue

dark blue

gold

sky blue

dark blue

gold

red

red

white

support

Fig. 37

Fig. 38

Incan Mask

Making the mask pictured in Fig. 39 also requires the use of a wooden support stand. See page 24 for instructions.

This mask was inspired by a famous ancient, Incan feathered serpent which was carved on temple facades. For your mask to be authentic, you should paint this sacred animal, using red, black and white as the dominant colors.

The base of this mask is a curved cardboard triangle M. Cut out appropriate holes for the eyes, nose and mouth to correspond to your own.

Surround this triangle with cardboard "feathers" which you can staple or glue to

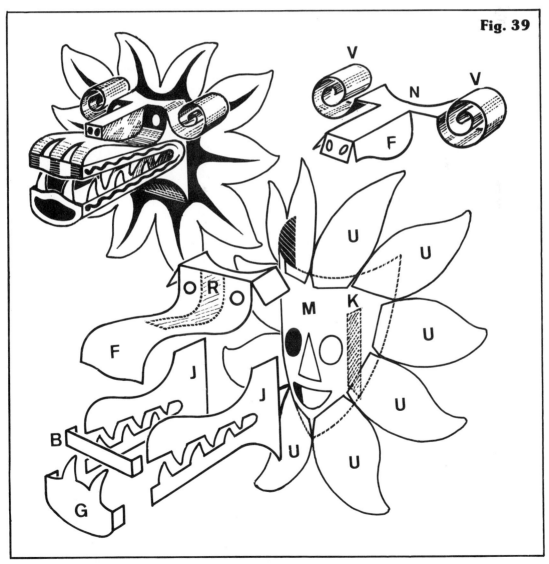

Fig. 39

the background (see pieces U, U, U, and so on). Bend the feathers forward so that they frame the muzzle.

The muzzle is essentially composed of two cheeks, J and J, solidly glued to the side areas marked K. You can determine exact separation between J pieces by how you attach strip B and the chin G. Then cover the muzzle with piece F, which has holes pierced in it for the eyes, and which you can appropriately curve to cover the muzzle. Secure the assembly of all the pieces with squares of gummed kraft paper which you attach from the inside.

All that remains is for you to make the nose N, which you fit with two curls V and V glued to piece F. Glue the nose to the streaked area marked R.

You can decorate this Incan mask by glueing on pieces of colored paper or bits of felt. You can use water-base paints, but the overall effect will not be nearly as brilliant.

Fig. 63 (p. 48) shows another interpretation of this Incan mask, but the construction is much more difficult than for the mask just described.

African Mask

This African sorcerer's mask breaks down into seven pieces that you assemble on a curved triangular background. The measurements shown in the pattern in Fig. 42 represent those of the original mask. Obviously, the size of your mask will differ according to your own measurements. The circumference of your head and the placement of your eyes are the two most important dimensions.

To create this mask, you need to use a support stand such as the one described earlier (see page 24).

Before you attempt to read the pattern in Fig. 42, note that the thick black lines are the cutting lines; the thick dotted lines are the fold lines; and the fine, continuous lines indicate the outlines of the decoration. The dotted and dashed lines marked with letters indicate where to glue the various elements together. You can easily draw the entire mask on a piece of bristol board or very heavy paper, 20 × 26 inches (50 × 65 cm). The mask shown here was drawn on a piece of bright red cardboard.

You must draw the base piece for this mask very carefully. Cut out holes for the eyes and mouth. Slit the nose with two strokes of a knife, and then raise up the sides, following the fold lines. Draw lines C-D-E, X-Y and M-N-O-P precisely.

Attach the foundation to your wooden stand, using two thumbtacks near the upper corners of the curved triangle. Be sure that the cardboard or paper face projects about three fingers' width above the support.

Glue two equal halves of a cork on to the two small circles marked B and B. These

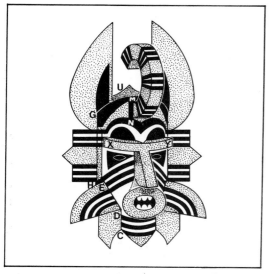

Fig. 40

Fig. 41

support the mouth on top of the mask foundation. Be sure to use glue that will hold these and the remaining parts in place. If necessary, you can reinforce the back of the glued area with small pieces of gummed kraft paper. These dry instantly and can be of great help.

Make two symmetrical ears, following the diagram in the bottom right-hand corner of Fig. 42. To give the ears sufficient rigidity, curve them towards the back of the vertical edge, in the form of a spout (see the two white arrows in the diagram). Be sure that the slit for interlocking the parts, G, is exactly the same thickness as the paper you are using. Note that in order to connect the ears, the mask must project beyond the top of the wooden stand by about 2 inches (5 cm). Line G-H shows the location of the connection.

In the same manner, cut out and fold two of the pattern pieces shown in the upper right-hand corner of Fig. 42. Place these pieces along the broken line C-D-E on either side of the mouth. Line D-E curves when the mask is shaped on the stand.

The pattern in the middle of Fig. 42 is for the horns, which ornament the middle of the forehead. In assembling this part, curve the long, straight strip and glue it edge-to-edge with the two curved side parts. Use small squares of gummed paper or adhesive tape to hold the pieces together; see the small diagram that illustrates this. The three points on the bottom serve to attach the horn to the mask, around square M-N-O-P.

The diagram in the bottom left-hand corner of Fig. 42 is for the nose, which is lengthened by the protruding eyebrows. The only difficulty with this part is in drawing curve Z correctly, so that you can attach it precisely to the mask. The exact degree of this curve depends on the degree to which the mask's stand is tilted. The given radius dimension of R = 22 inches (55 cm) is thus only approximate.

Fig. 40 shows how to decorate this mask. The cutouts are enhanced with white water-base paint and glued-on black strips. You could also paint the black areas. The rest of the mask (dotted in Fig. 40) is blood red.

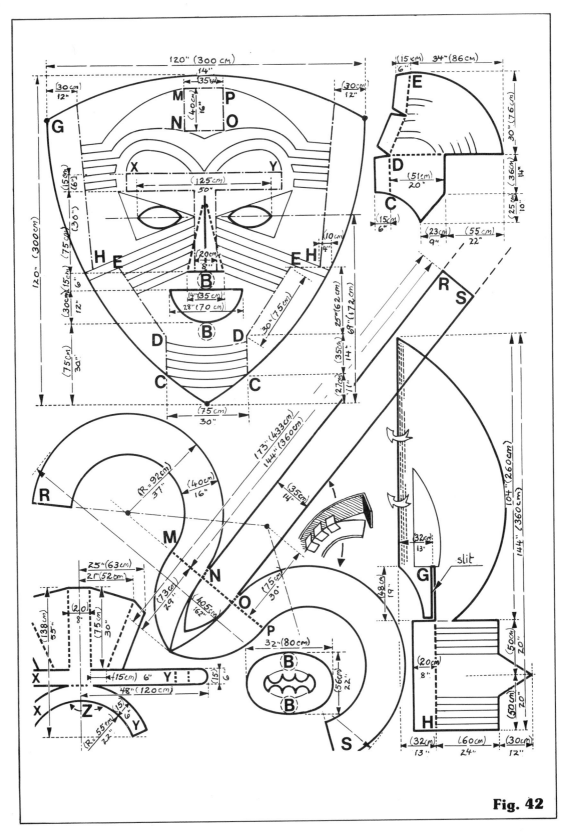

Fig. 42

Sudanese Sorcerer's Mask

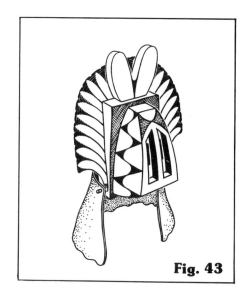

Fig. 43

Here is a paper-and-cardboard interpretation of an African mask housed in the Museum of Man in Paris. It is a mask from the Dogon region of the Sudan and is completely painted ochre, black and white (see Fig. 43).

The original mask is made of lightweight wood and is completely hollowed out to hold the head of the wearer. The central block is topped with a pair of ears or horns and a kind of crown frames it, forming a mane.

The shoulders and neck of the wearer of this mask are covered with a type of cloak. You can replace this part with lots of long strands of raffia knotted around a long cord.

Constructing the mask

1. The pattern for the main part of the mask, U, is given in Fig. 45. It looks like an incomplete box, resembling a shovel or a scoop. The bottom of this box is mostly hollow and forms an archway through which the head of the wearer can pass. If you look at Fig. 44, you can see that the

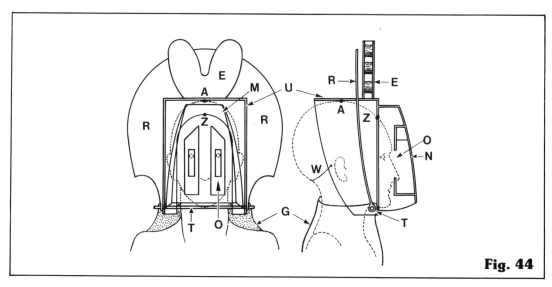

Fig. 44

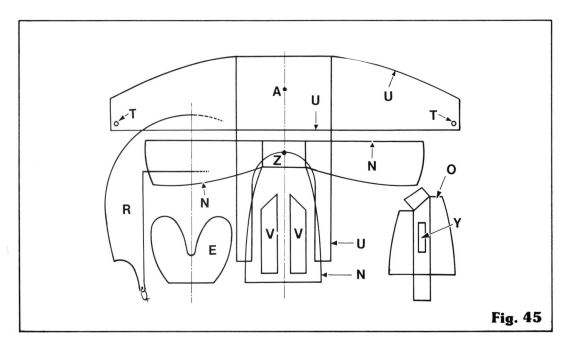

Fig. 45

top of your head will touch the box at point A and that your forehead will touch the archway at point Z. To hold this construction in place, pass a thin stick of light wood under your chin and through two holes T and T in the box. Attach a piece of string or elastic to this stick to hold the mask behind the nape of your neck.

2. A second pattern piece N forms the "muzzle." Cut out two large slits in N (V and V), as shown in Fig. 45.

Assemble parts U and N from the inside, using strips of adhesive cloth or tape; you can also use gummed kraft paper. Then connect U and N to each other in the same manner.

3. Fold and assemble two parts O, shown in Fig. 45. Cut vertical slits Y opposite your eyes into each O piece. Attach the O pieces to the V's.

4. Cut out two identical pieces shaped like E and attach them to each other by glueing equal slices of cork between them. This also ensures that the two parts of the horns are parallel. You can hide the cork

with a long contour of tape that completely covers the space between them. Solidly glue the horns in place.

5. All that remains is to cut the crown from very thick paper, following the half pattern R in Fig. 45. Decorate this piece, following Fig. 43. Attach it in place, well spread out, to the ends of the stick T.

6. Now put the little cloak in place. The easiest way to make this piece is to cut it out from a piece of felt.

Attractively painted in ochre, black and white, this mask is truly striking.

Animal Masks

The difficulty in making animal masks is in shaping the dominant form of the snout or muzzle.

Use fairly flexible cardboard or a piece of old linoleum; to begin, cut out pieces *a*, *b*, *c* and *d* following Fig. 46. The sizes of these pieces, as well as the shape of the ears, depends on which animal you plan to depict.

Sew the various pieces together with fine thread, then glue the joints from the inside. When the glue is completely dry, cut the thread carefully from the outside.

Glue the eyes *e* on separately and paint them appropriate colors.

If your animal requires whiskers, refer to diagram *m*. Thread a piece of semiflexible electrical wire through two holes as shown.

Fig. 46

Also notice the hole pierced in piece *c*. Line this hole up with your eyes, so that you can see out when you are wearing your mask.

Another procedure you can follow to make an animal mask is to use spread fasteners to attach a piece such as *f* to an ordinary mask such as *g*. Using similar fasteners, attach a bottom piece *i*, into which you cut out a tongue as shown. The end of the muzzle *h* joins part *f* and *i* in front.

All that remains is to glue a series of cardboard strips *j*, *k*, *l* and *n* on to the mask. You can cover these strips with pieces of colored crepe paper to form the animal's hide. Attach long strips of paper *p* to form a mane.

Fig. 47 shows some variations of the basic animal pattern just described.

Fig. 47

A Simple Mask

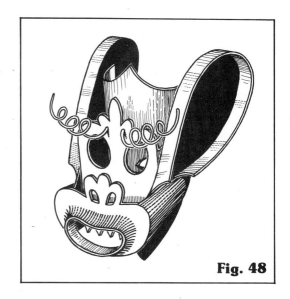

Fig. 48

To make the mask pictured in Fig. 48, you need a wooden stand (see page 24). Using thumbtacks, attach the foundation piece M, curved into shape, to this stand.

Connect the various pieces and armatures that comprise the different relief surfaces and angles of this mask to this foundation. Begin by glueing a cork B and a cardboard stirrup E to M (see Figs. 48, 49 and 50). Be sure to use a rapidly drying glue.

Piece F forms the face. Cut out the holes for the eyes, as shown in the drawings. Glue this piece inside the stirrup E and on top of the cork B. In the middle of F, glue another cork B. Be sure to place this second cork even with the front part of E.

Now attach shape G (the muzzle) in front. If you wish, you can complete the muzzle with a cardboard strip R, which you can curve appropriately and glue around the mouth. Connect the ends of this curve by glueing on a paper covering (see Fig. 48).

Now glue two ears K to the sides of the head. You can give the ears more of a relief effect by adding strips such as L around each one.

Complete the relief by adding the cheeks J, which you can construct from strips of gummed paper spread around G and attached behind M. Cover these strips with a piece of paper that is cut to fit exactly over them.

You do not, of course, need to copy exactly the simple design suggested here. You can vary the shapes of the cutouts (the forehead, ears and snout, for example) or

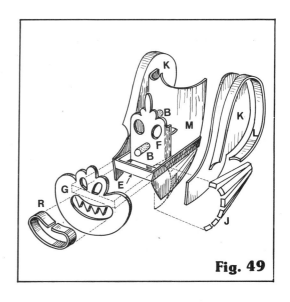

Fig. 49

you can change the proportions and length of the pieces, especially the muzzle. You can also improve the shape of your mask by closing up some of the holes separating the various parts, using easy-to-make paper coverings.

Whatever shape your animal mask takes, you need to decorate it after you have it assembled. On a piece of paper, trace and cut out the various pattern pieces. Use these patterns to cut out different pieces of colorful felt to glue on to the parts of the mask. You can paint the mask with matt-finish paints instead.

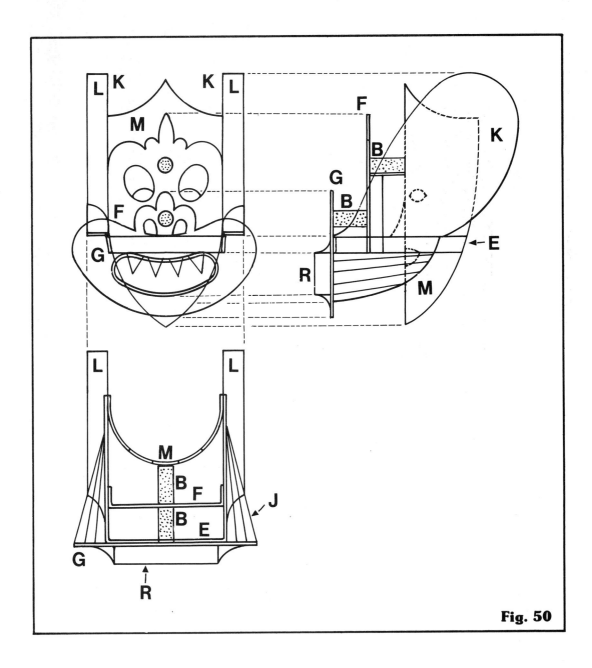

Fig. 50

Deer Mask

The support for the background of this deer is a curved rectangle Z. After cutting out two eye sockets U (see Figs. 51 and 52), attach two side pieces M to Z.

Next place the large piece F-N-T from the top of the forehead to the end of the snout. Keep the inside of this mask hollow so that you can fit your head in and be heard when you speak.

Cut out pieces O for the ears. Reinforce each ear with a vein P, which you glue on from behind.

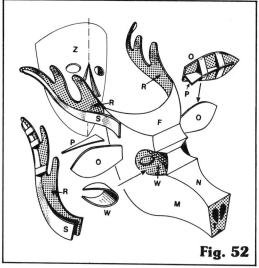

Fig. 52

Assemble all the pieces of this mask by using small squares of gummed kraft paper, which dry immediately.

Now insert a curved piece W into each eye socket, also using small squares of gummed paper. Cut out these W pieces to fit exactly inside the eye holes you already made.

Next, cut out strips of newsprint and dunk them into some paste. Cover the already assembled parts of your mask with these wet strips, one layer at a time; when one layer has dried, add another. Let dry and then add a third layer. When this paper covering has dried completely, paint the mask beige.

Next, make the deer's antlers. To begin this delicate procedure, cut out pieces R and S. You will attach them to each other along the dotted line shown in Fig. 51. To attach R and S perpendicularly to each other, wind strips of gummed kraft paper around them, as shown in Fig. 52. Cover over the resulting triangular areas between the two pieces with a piece of paper. Notice in the drawings that little by little, towards the bottom, piece S becomes parallel to R, twisting progressively towards the point. This enables you to insert and glue the edge of the mask between R and S.

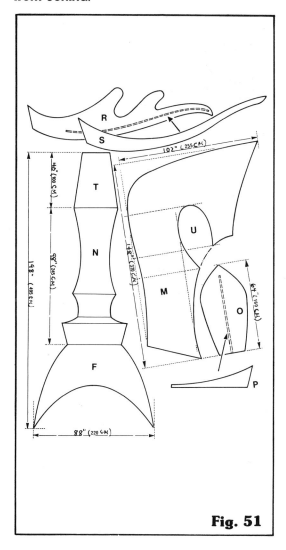

Fig. 51

Big, Bad Wolf

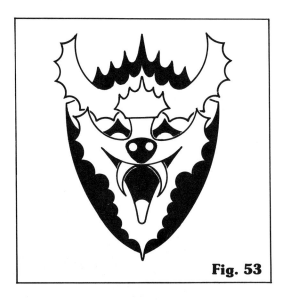

Fig. 53

To make the mask pictured in Fig. 53, mount a lightweight cardboard, curved triangle J on a stand, as·shown in Fig. 54. With strong glue, attach stirrups A (on the forehead), C (in front of the mouth) and D (in front of the eyes) to this background.

Next cut out the main piece M (see Fig. 56), which you fold in two places to form the two planes of this mask. Glue the upper level of M (the ears) to stirrup A and the lower level (the mouth) to stirrup C. Attach part E to the horizontal area that forms the snout at line X-Y.

Note that you can also glue on wedges of cork J and K to facilitate assembling this mask. Fig. 55 shows the location of the various elements of this project. Notice that piece C has holes cut in it to receive strips of raffia or ribbon R.

Cut out piece D. Notice that D has a

tongue L in the middle to glue under the snout on piece M. Make the fangs from a crescent N. Glue it inside the mouth.

Fig. 57 shows the mask completely assembled. Note that no decorations are indicated in the drawing. This is so that you can clearly see the shapes. You should build this mask without thinking about the coloration at all; decide how to decorate it after it is made. There are many methods you can use: You can paint it with water-base paints, or you can glue on a collage of colored tissue, crepe paper or pieces of felt. The mask pictured here was inspired by a photograph of a fox. However, it is not difficult to modify the fox pattern slightly to create a bear, a jackal or even a tiger. Find a good photograph of any of these animals, cut your pattern pieces to correspond and then color your mask.

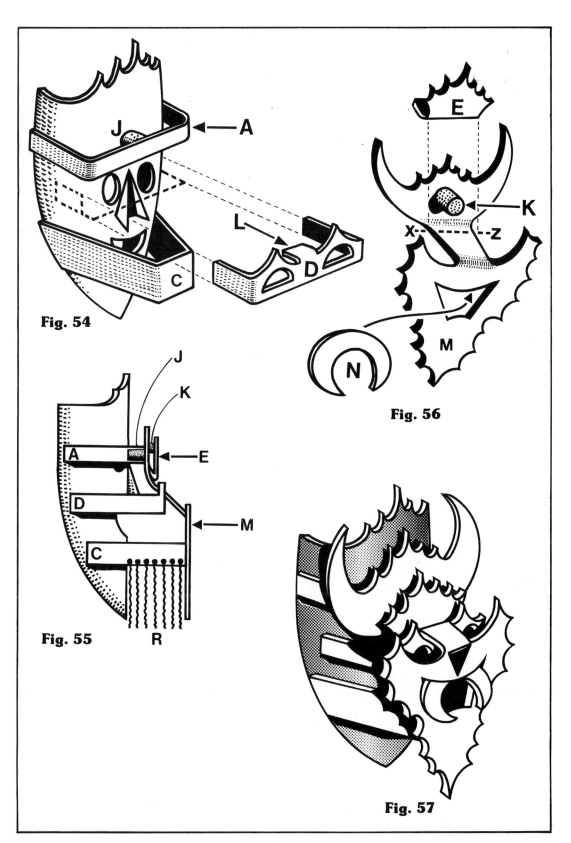

Fig. 54

Fig. 55

Fig. 56

Fig. 57

Ram Mask

To begin this project, draw full-size patterns of both the front view of the face and the profile of this mask (see Fig. 58) on a piece of brown paper. You can refer to these drawings for certain essential measurements while you work.

Attach the backplate S for this mask to a wooden stand and curve it as previously described. Secure the snout by glueing the two pieces M and N vertically along the middle axis of S. You can see that if you vary the width, length and curvature of the muzzle parts, you can create all sorts of different animals.

Now glue a series of cork slices down each side of the mask. Notice in Fig. 58 that these cork pieces (C, C and C) are arranged with the longest one on top and the thinnest on the bottom.

Cut out two pieces of cardboard P. Curve them so they fit exactly along the edges of piece M. Attach these P pieces to the cork slices with thumbtacks. Join angles M-P with small gummed-paper hinges glued one next to the other (not shown in Fig. 58 so as to simplify the drawing). You should have an empty space left between S and P; this widens the head.

Now, determine the correct placement for the eyes. Cut out the holes in the support S. Then draw and hollow out the eye sockets Q. Finally, measuring the length of the edges of these sockets, cut out curved cardboard spindles R. Mark the correct placement for the eye holes; then, with a large hole-puncher, pierce an eye hole in each R.

Attach these fit-to-order pieces R along the edges of the hollows marked Q. Hold them in place with hinges made from adhesive tape or gummed paper.

The skull is finished; the horns must now be added. Depending on the direction and general placement of the horns, you can make masks for any number of different animals—perhaps a deer, doe or ox. Simply flatten the end of the muzzle, for example.

Fig. 59 illustrates the assembly of the horns. Begin by glueing the forehead piece F to the top of the snout M. Connect this to the top edge of the mask.

Make the horns in three segments. First glue pieces D and D (by the streaked part shown in Fig. 59) to the front of M. Use a glue that dries quickly. Reinforce the seams with strips of adhesive tape, if necessary. When D and M are well connected, join the edges of F and D to create the desired contour. Next attach the G pieces behind P. Use gummed-paper hinges or adhesive tape to do this.

Join the tips of D and G, using a small curl E made from gummed paper. These pieces E extend the forehead F to the edges of the horns. The close-up diagram in the lower left-hand corner of Fig. 59 shows how to connect the different angles of this mask.

After you have finished assembling all these parts, you must paper over the entire construction with several thicknesses of newsprint strips that are drenched with glue. This serves to thicken and strengthen the lightweight cardboard that you used as the foundation of this mask; do not make this paper covering more than one-quarter of an inch (1 mm) thicker than the original cardboard. This papering technique also covers up the small bumps caused by the connections you formed in assembling the mask.

Let the glue-and-paper covering dry until the newsprint is quite hard and white. Lightly sand any remaining blemishes or

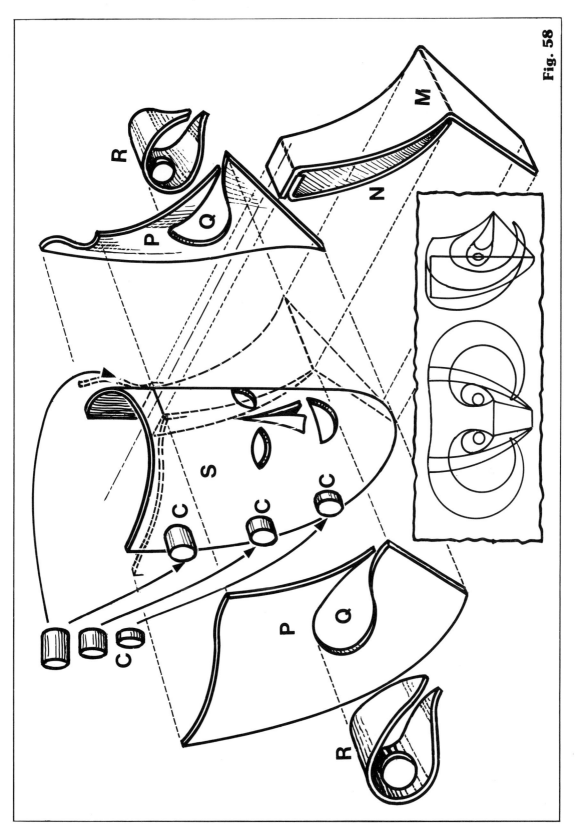

Fig. 58

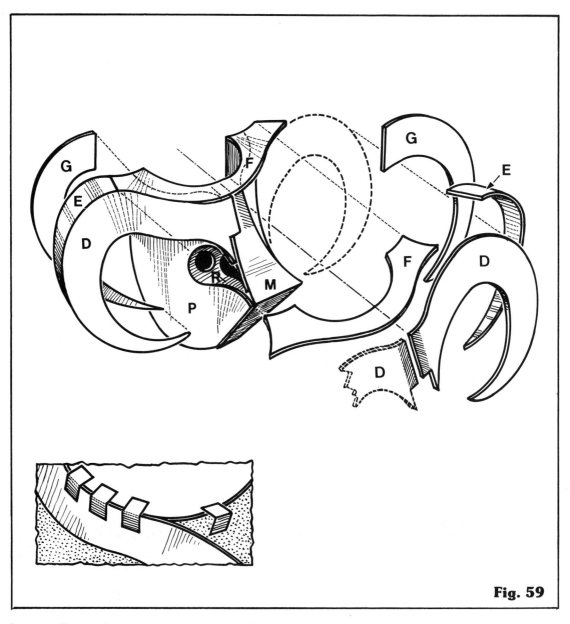

Fig. 59

bumps. Cover the entire construction with a coat of matt paint. This serves as a foundation for the colorful cutout felt decorations that you now apply. Instead of felt, you can glue colored pieces of paper to the painted surface or you can paint additional designs with water-base paints.

This technique for mask-making requires no special materials; making the mask this way is much cleaner than if modelling clay were used. Besides, the rigidity of cardboard encourages you to experiment artistically and to discover ways to simplify shapes and curves.

Mask from the
Ivory Coast

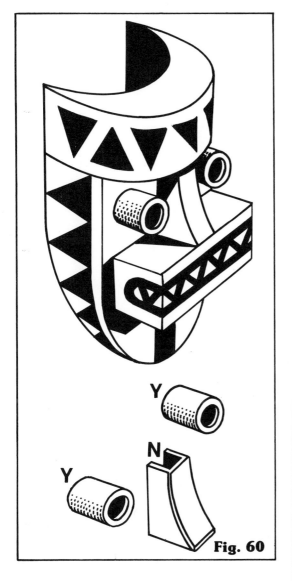

Fig. 60

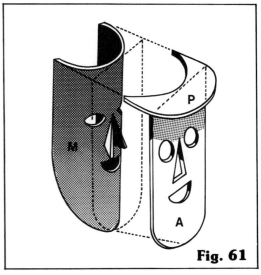

Fig. 61

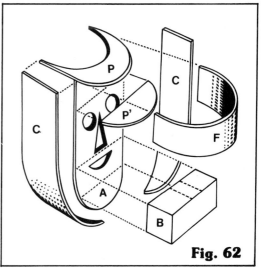

Fig. 62

Another Incan Mask

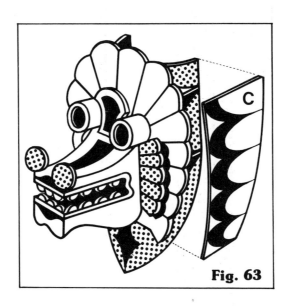

Fig. 63

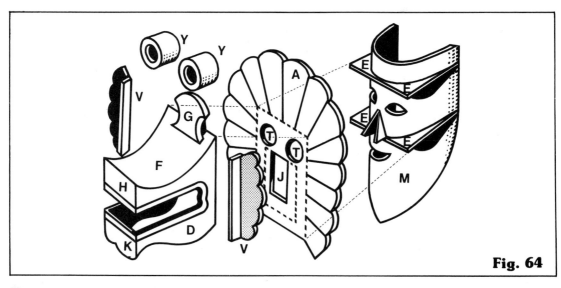

Fig. 64

Moulded Masks

It is possible that you might want or need several copies of the same mask. You might also wish to preserve a mask you have produced after a long trial session with modelling clay. In either case, the only solution is to make a plaster mould.

To begin with, a clay model involves dimension. You must be very careful that all the protruding parts of the model remain intact—that is, you must painstakingly remove the plaster from the clay mould so that you do not leave any pieces behind.

When you have finished your clay model, grease it carefully. Surround the clay model with several vertical boards to keep it steady, and fill the model with plaster. When the plaster mould is dry, line it with glue-soaked layers of newspaper. Let each layer of paper dry before you add the next. When two or three layers have dried, unmould the paper. Paint and decorate the mask.

Decorating a Mask

The shapes shown in Fig. 65 represent an excellent exercise to help you discover a suitable decoration for a mask.

To make masks such as these, you simply cut two or even three pieces of colored paper. When you glue the pieces together side by side, the result is a face whose expression and style you can vary. If you use this technique, you are not obliged to portray realistic features, such as eyes, nose or mouth. Instead, you can simply create an overall image.

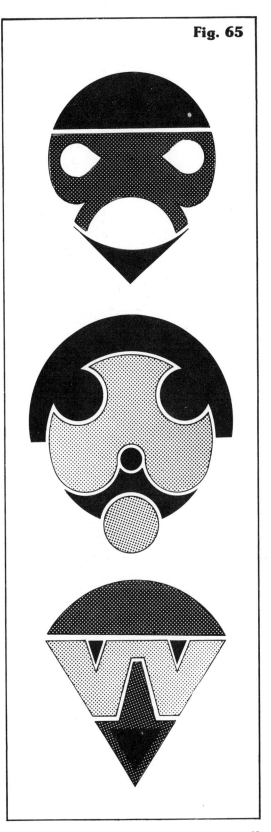

Fig. 65

Fig. 66

Finger and Hand Puppets

PUPPETS

Before you begin . . .

A puppet is a finely tuned instrument that blends shape and color in motion. It is a visual instrument, just as the pipe, drum and organ are sound instruments. However, only specially trained craftspeople can make musical instruments, whether they are stringed, reed or percussion. Furthermore, to become a violinist, a flutist, a pianist, an organist or a kettledrummer, a student needs to study and practice for many hours. For the puppeteer, nothing of the sort is necessary! Different puppets made by special artists are commercially available, but sometimes these may not meet your individual requirements. So, *you* must become your own instrument-maker; *you* can make your own puppets.

Puppets are often still considered to be mere children's toys. Thus, they usually exhibit only ordinary actions and when clothed, often look like gawky penguins.

However, it is from the puppet's role as a simplistic children's toy that the strength of its rebirth came. A puppet combines shape, color, movement, language, visual and musical rhythms—it is a live toy that can express as many things as you wish. A puppet can learn . . . understand . . . suggest . . . rouse.

Consider who and what you would like your puppet to be, and use your hands to translate your thoughts into working puppets. It is hoped that the ideas in this book

will help you create—as if by magic—
live, active personalities from ordinary and
readily available materials.

Hand puppets

A very primitive hand puppet is composed of a head attached to a stick. Long
ago, the King's jester carried such a puppet, as the King carried his sceptre. The
jester depended on this puppet to dictate
his silly antics. As a result, frivolity was
associated with most early puppets, as well
as with puppets in old engravings.

Today, such puppets have been revived
and used as a form of entertainment. They
can often be found in children's parks and
nursery schools, where they are used to
illustrate songs and games, accompanied
by musical instruments or records. Manipulating these puppets is simple; merely follow the rhythm and melody of the music.

Trying to imitate a marching rhythm or
what can be considered the walk of certain
animals greatly changed these primitive
puppets, because puppeteers were forced
to hold the puppets with two hands and to
train their right hands to ignore what their
left hands were doing. Such two-sticked
creations were the great-grandparents of
today's puppets.

Huge dolls mounted on stems, which do
not require the hands to penetrate under a
costume, can also be classified as puppets.
Such dolls exhibit much expression.

In the same way, the *wayang goleck*
from Java can be considered to be a
puppet. The *wayang* is mounted on a
finely carved stick that forms the body and
supports and connects to the head, which it
turns. The arms are also formed from sticks
attached at the cross-stick that forms the
shoulders. The hands are supported, held
up and animated by two long and sometimes finely carved sticks made of wood,
bone or ivory.

Fig. 67

Fig. 68

Fig. 69

Fig. 70

Sleeve puppets

A sleeve puppet consists of a head and a sleeve covering. The sleeve, a glove or glovelike covering worn on the hand of the puppeteer, becomes the body of the puppet. It is the sheath that commands the puppet and controls the visible movements of the character. In this type of puppet, the personality comes from within the puppet's body.

The large variety of sleeve puppets divides into several groups, depending on the type of sheath. Following are some of the different sleeve characters you can make.

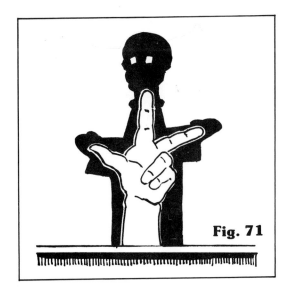

Fig. 71

Fig. 72

A Russian character

The smallest sleeve puppet is the Russian type, which is composed of a sleeve that ends in a three-pointed star. The sleeve is slightly conical and covers the forearm from the wrist to the elbow.

The puppeteer's hand penetrates into the three points of the star: The index finger goes into the topmost point, and the thumb and the middle finger go into the other two, creating a very flexible body.

The head remains completely independent of the body. You add it just when the puppet is ready to act (see Fig. 74).

Fig. 75

Fig. 73

Fig. 76

Fig. 74

A German character

You can create a German puppet (Fig. 75), based on the same principle as the Russian one (flexibility), but leave the topmost point of the star open to receive the head. You can sink your fingers directly into this opening to manipulate the puppet (see Fig. 76). You also use your fingers to form the arms of the puppet. Cover the ends of the arms with cloth hands into which you insert your fingers.

Fig. 77

An Italian character

The Italian "Buratino" is a large doll. The head is supported by a small stick that your middle finger, fourth finger and little finger turn against the palm of your hand. Your index finger and thumb remain free to manipulate the leather cones that direct the hands.

The body, which forms a support for the clothes, has two slits in the front into which you insert the cones that form the arms (see Fig. 77).

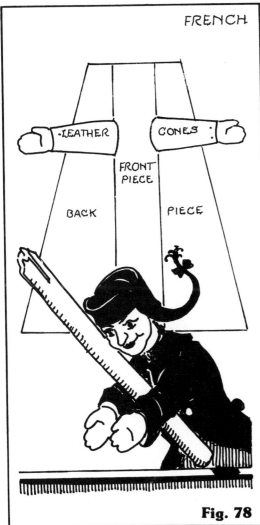

Fig. 78

A French character

The French puppet is almost a direct offspring of the Italian puppet described above. The body is short and wide and consists of four pieces: one narrow strip onto which you attach two independent pieces for the cylindrical arms, and a large piece that forms the back (see Fig. 78).

Make the entire costume for this large puppet from fairly stiff material. The hands are wooden and are furnished with conical leather arms which permit you to manoeuver the puppet.

Because these dolls are so stiff, their actions resemble those of finger puppets, even though they are flexible enough to pick up, hit and turn around like other sheathed puppets.

You manipulate this type of puppet differently from those described earlier; instead of using only your middle finger where discussed for the previous puppets, you use your middle finger, fourth finger and little finger. The inside of the puppet contains no bent-back fingers.

An English character

An English puppet is often constructed like the French one. However, you can also wear it like the German puppet, using only three fingers. The costume for the English puppet is also less complicated to make than that of the Italian or French puppet, because, as you can see in Fig. 79, it is simply composed of three straight strips of fabric.

Fig. 80

A Spanish character

You can easily create a Spanish puppet, because all that differentiates a "royal" Spaniard from a "noble" Frenchman is that you hold the head of the doll by the index finger, the middle finger and the fourth finger, thus leaving your thumb and little finger free to animate the arms.

This manner of manipulation allows you to use your two hands to animate two characters at once. It also allows the doll's head to turn almost as easily as that of the Italian puppet described previously.

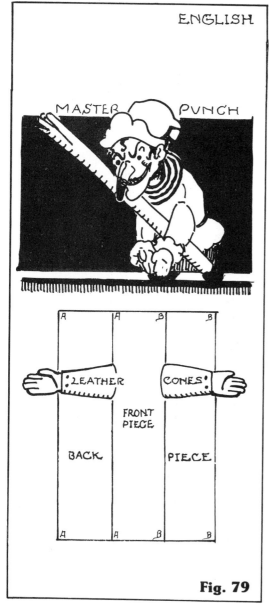

Fig. 79

The various ideas for the international costumes described are not absolute. Puppeteers have always modified the "laws" of puppet-making to satisfy their own needs and convenience. As if surgically, such craftspeople have created perfectly acceptable variations which enrich the "orchestra" of puppets with new "tones." Recently, certain forgotten puppet-making principles have been revived for creating simple finger and sleeve puppets as well.

The head

All puppets you can make have one part of the body in common: the head. Whether you make the head of wood, plaster, silk or cardboard; whether you carve it, mould it, stamp it or cast it, you must be sure your puppet's head is lightweight.

But it must never be completely hollow. No matter what material you use, if the head is heavier than the weight of your hand, you must partially hollow out its crown. Be careful how much you hollow out, because your hand should never sink or disappear into an entirely empty space.

Your hand should never be able to penetrate into the head farther than your second knuckle. To ensure that you never stick your fingers into an empty space, construct a narrow, cone-shaped connection between the body and the head. You can either hollow out this area just inside the head from the material from which you made the head, or you can make a hollow separately from papier-mâché and insert it into the wood, cardboard or cloth head. See Fig. 81. (You do not need to hollow out the head of puppets, mobile or not, whose bodies you attach to central stems.)

Remember when decorating the head that puppets are not meant to imitate people, but to "evoke" feelings. The features can, however, be completely realistic so that the audience can recognize a particular temperament.

Carving a head out of wood allows you to create a variety of different characters easily. Using papier-mâché, on the other hand, is much more difficult. You can easily adorn your first puppet creations with painted or embroidered cloth for rapid results.

Now, let us begin . . .

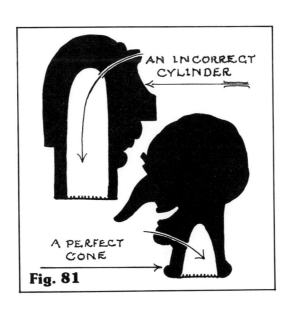

AN INCORRECT CYLINDER

A PERFECT CONE

Fig. 81

WOODEN
HEADS

Fig. 82

GLUE

PAPIER-
MÂCHÉ

Fig. 83

Fig. 84

Fig. 85

Glove Finger Puppets

It is never too early to introduce children to decorating and working with various materials. For example, you can pique their interest in puppet-making by teaching them to make the small paper people shown in Figs. 86 and 87.

Making finger puppets is a wonderful pastime for the young and old alike. You only need a few materials to begin: some lightweight bristol board or heavyweight paper in a variety of colors; gummed paper; scissors, some glue and a sharp knife.

Fig. 86

Fig. 87

Each puppet consists of a long cone of rolled paper. Roll each piece of paper to exactly fit the finger on which you plan to wear the puppet. Make two slits opposite each other through which you attach the arms. That is all there is to it! The rest of the task is a matter of personal taste. Use as much imagination as you like for decorating your character. Your choice of colors is certainly very important, whether you use colored paper or you plan to paint the puppet after it is finished.

You can also create puppets entirely from heavy white paper. Such puppets can perform in a specially decorated cardboard box, which serves as a small theatre, or you can animate your personalities between a screen and a movie projector, which enlarges the shadows cast by the dolls. This also enables your creations to perform in front of a larger audience.

If you want, you can make finger puppets that are bigger than the diameter of a single finger. To do this, you need to join two paper trumpets, one inside the other, and connect them at the top. The inner tube should fit securely around your finger; the second sits on top of the first somewhat like a lampshade. This top tube can be any dimension you wish. In this way, you can create a variety of figures on cones with very large bases.

Very young children can have a wonderful time with this project: you can assemble the cones ahead of time, add the arms as previously described, and let each child decorate the prefabricated puppet as he or she wishes—the idea is to transform the flat roll of paper into a three-dimensional personality!

Fig. 88

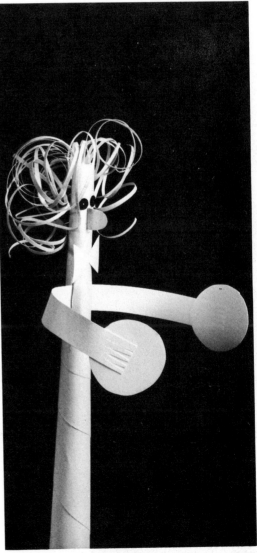

Decorating on a Dummy

How you decorate your puppets is an important aspect of creating their personalities. Here is an exercise to familiarize you with fanciful costuming. First, construct a dummy. Follow Fig. 89, and cut out shapes B (arms) and D (head) from wood about half an inch (15 mm) thick.

Thread the arms B on to a bar of round wood A, which is supported on a base S. Shape a thick tube of cardboard C, slit it as shown at F, cut out a hole T to fit around the bar A and thread it on A to round out the shoulders of the dummy. Drill or carve out a hole in the head D, so that the head can move even after threaded onto A. The

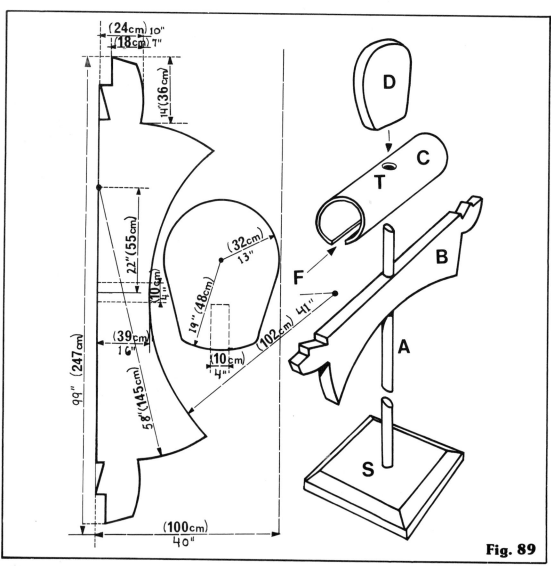

Fig. 89

Fig. 90

total height of the dummy should be equal to seven or eight heads.

Making the costume

Drape a long strip of paper with a hole in its middle over the shoulders you have just constructed so that it hangs in front and in back of the base, like a stole. Glue various shapes cut from colored paper to ornament this piece of paper like a cloak. Using your imagination, arrange and rearrange the cutouts to create a decoration that is appealing. The design does not necessarily

have to have a realistic look to it.

When the decoration is well in place, in a design that you like, reproduce the paper cutouts from a strip of felt placed flat on the table. Glue on these multicolored pieces of felt wherever you wish.

You can complete this project by adding a hairstyle that complements the character's outfit. For the face, you can allow for the eyes, but be careful not to detail all the facial features so as to leave some features to the viewers' imaginations.

This work is an excellent introduction to decorating puppets. It is especially interesting because it is three-dimensional.

Rod Puppets

Some people think that puppet-making is an activity that adults do for children and that children do not do for themselves. Sometimes, however, a teacher can help even very young children to use the technique described in this section to create marvelous puppets. The process described here really only involves cutting out and pasting colored papers, which are usually flat.

The teacher's part in making these hand puppets (which do not have arms) consists of preparing the simple wooden rods or supports. Each puppet consists of a rectangular or trapezoidal head nailed to a lightweight wooden stem (Fig. 91). Fig. 91 also shows how you can add a cylindrical or cone-shaped head made from very flexible cardboard or drawing paper to these rods. Nail these shapes to the cross section of the rod after appropriately curving them.

Using supports such as these, you can create an entire crowd of people who vary in their coloration and style. You can paint your finished creations with water-base paints or glue on colored paper or felt cutouts. Figs. 92 and 93 show you some examples. You can make the nose, ears—even a plain or fancy hairstyle— using any materials you wish.

If you are making a rod puppet for a young child to decorate, ask the child to

Fig. 91

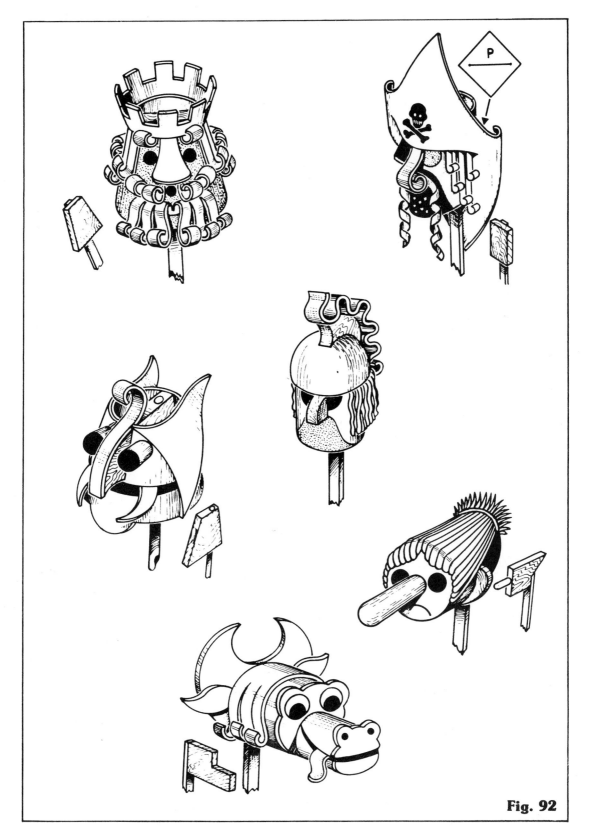

P

Fig. 92

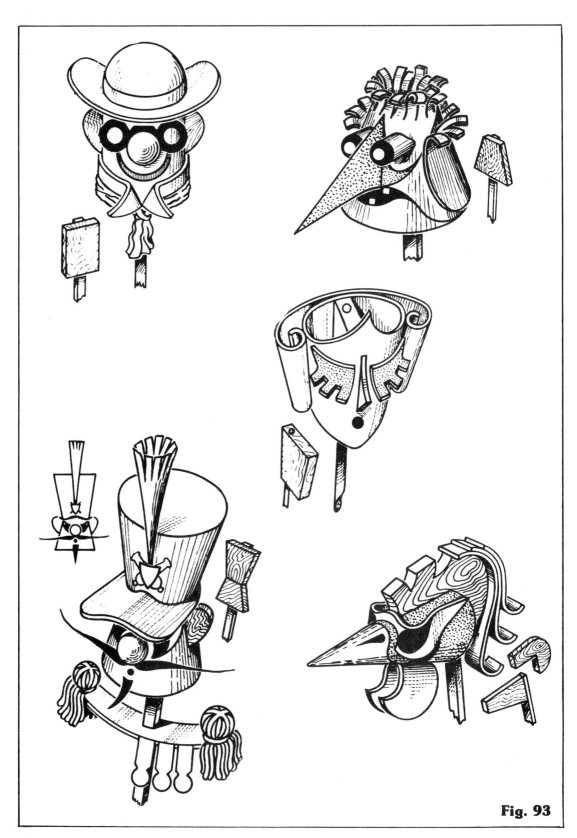

Fig. 93

68

Fig. 94

help choose the shape. Make a small drawing for the child to use as a guide while completing the project. Be sure that the small diagram is only a guide and that it does not prevent the artist from improvising while he or she works. The final creation might even be quite different from the original plan.

You can dress these puppets simply by using a large square piece of cloth, tightened with a cord around the neck. The puppeteer holds the puppet by the stem, which is under this cloth. If you wish, you can broaden your puppet's shoulders by adding a crosspiece at the height of the shoulders; then drape the fabric over this support.

This simple and tidy technique for making puppets is ideal for young children. It can also be invaluable for creative but busy adults who do not have the leisure time necessary for sculpting, modelling or sewing more complicated puppets.

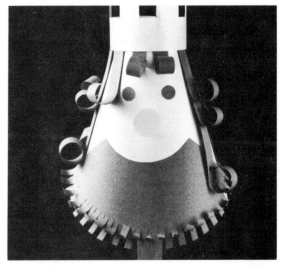

Fig. 95

Walking Dolls

These charming little toys are related to the puppet family. After you learn how to make these miniature people, you can enjoy animating their personalities since their legs consist of two of your fingers. You can make your dolls dance on a table, sit down, stand up, straddle obstacles, climb on top of things in an exaggerated, comical way—anything you wish them to do to entertain your audience.

Making a walking doll is very simple. You begin by attaching a lightweight head to the top of a lightweight torso (see Fig. 97). First make a cone 3 inches (7 cm) high from bristol board. Glue the edges of this cone C together or fasten them with adhesive tape from the inside. Next, attach a flat oval to the top of this cone (A in Fig. 97) to form the shoulders. Use adhesive tape cut into small squares to assemble these pieces (S in Fig. 97). Cut similar squares to reinforce the bottom edges of the bristol-board cone (see V in the diagram).

Make the head from a table-tennis ball that is about 1¼ inches (3 cm) in diameter. Glue the ball to the end of a piece of rattan (see B-R in Fig. 97). Thread the stem R through the oval A and glue it at U as shown.

Next use two spread fasteners P through two holes T to attach an elastic band ½ inch (15 mm) wide and 10 to 12 inches (25 to 30 cm) around to the back of the body at waist height. Wrap this elastic band

around your hand to manipulate the completed puppet.

Now dress and decorate this foundation, using small pieces of different colored felt. In this manner, you can make this doll into anyone you wish: a dancer, a soldier, an officer, an animal trainer, a cowboy, and so on.

Fig. 98 shows an example of a jacket with sleeves (M-N-Y) which is glued at the shoulders to a rattan cross-stick K. Make the hands for this costume from two thicknesses of felt which you glue to the inside of the cuff.

After you have finished this bust portion of your puppet, make the boots. First make the feet from two wooden soles D onto which you glue small round pieces of wood G, as shown. Next, roll a piece of heavyweight paper to form the tube H. The inside measurement of tube H should correspond to the size of your finger (or the finger of the puppeteer). The boots remain separate from the body and are worn like thimbles on the ends of two fingers.

Decorate the boots with assorted felt from the costume you made previously. Note pattern F in Fig. 97 for the piece of felt you will use to cover the feet; upholster the inside of the boots with a small scrap of felt. Glue F around the outside of the foot, cutting the edges with a razor blade. Leave the sole of the boot uncovered. This enables your puppet to produce a joyful tap dance on the tabletop.

To manoeuvre this puppet, you must put a black glove W on your working hand. Cut off the index and third fingers of the glove to create holes for the boots.

Fig. 99 shows how you should stretch the elastic band E around your hand and thumb to control the dancing doll.

Fig. 96

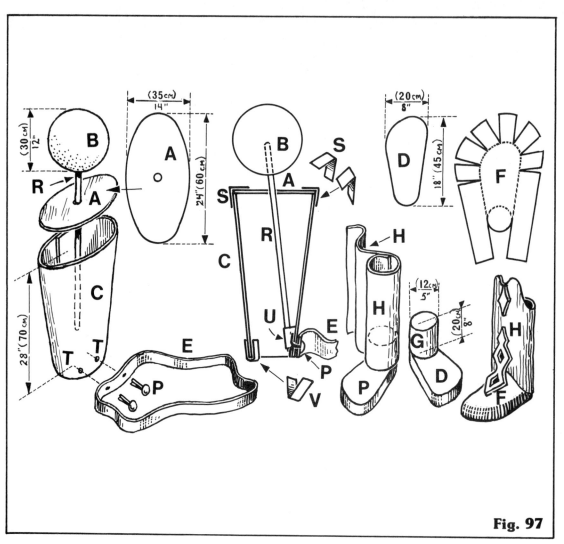

Fig. 97

Fig. 98

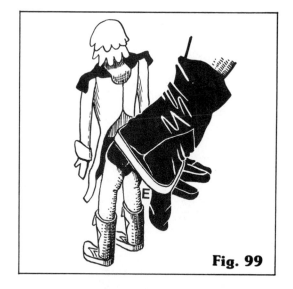

Fig. 99

Cardboard Puppets

Incidentally, manipulating these puppets is very easy. Even large dolls whose heads are about 5 or 6 inches (12 or 16 cm) are surprisingly lightweight.

This clever process for puppet-making allows you to reproduce almost exactly any model you have designed. You are not restricted to adding to a cone-shaped or cylindrical wooden base as has been previously described. In making this type of puppet, you can arrange in any way you wish the curves and angles that define your character's personality.

Making the head

This project is not at all messy; it does not require modelling with clay or lots of water to clean up with. You can easily make this project in a classroom or in a small area at home.

It is necessary, first of all, that you design the front view and the profile of the head you would like to create (see Fig. 100).

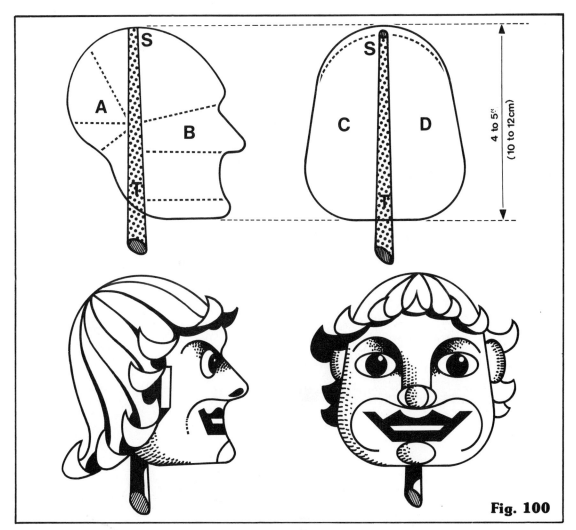

Fig. 100

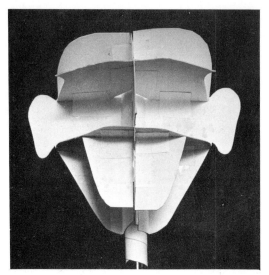

Fig. 101

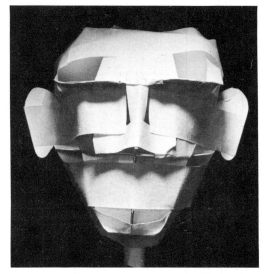

Fig. 102

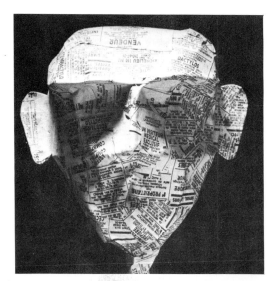

Fig. 103

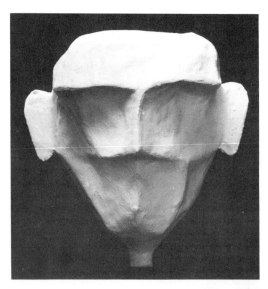

Fig. 104

tube at the neck to easily attach the body when the head is finished.

Imbed a strip of wood R into a bottle weighted down with sand W as shown in Fig. 107. Insert the other end of R into tube T. Now you can begin the armature.

Place the tube on your drawing and mark with pencil two lines that outline the edges of this tube. Then trace and cut out parts A and B for the profile and C and D of the face from lightweight cardboard. Assemble these pieces in a cross around tube T, using hinges made from gummed strips of kraft paper about 1 inch (25 mm) wide (see H in Fig. 107).

From this point on, your work varies for each different head you make, depending on the exterior shapes you intend to create.

Fig. 105

Then draw a simplified outline of the head in the exact dimensions that you want your finished project to be. You will find it easier to make a head that is not less than about 4 to 5 inches (10 to 12 cm) high. This also ensures that the puppet will be visible from the stage during a performance.

Now you make an armature around which you shape the head. Begin by rolling a piece of paper into an elongated tube T, which you reinforce with strips of adhesive tape K (see Fig. 107).

Place this tube onto your drawing. Cut the tube at E, following the incline S-S of the profile at this point. Also cut T at F as shown, making sure you can insert your finger into the tube at the point where you cut. You will use the projecting part of the

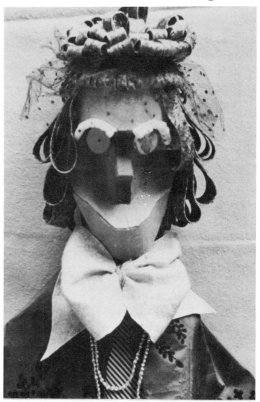

Fig. 106

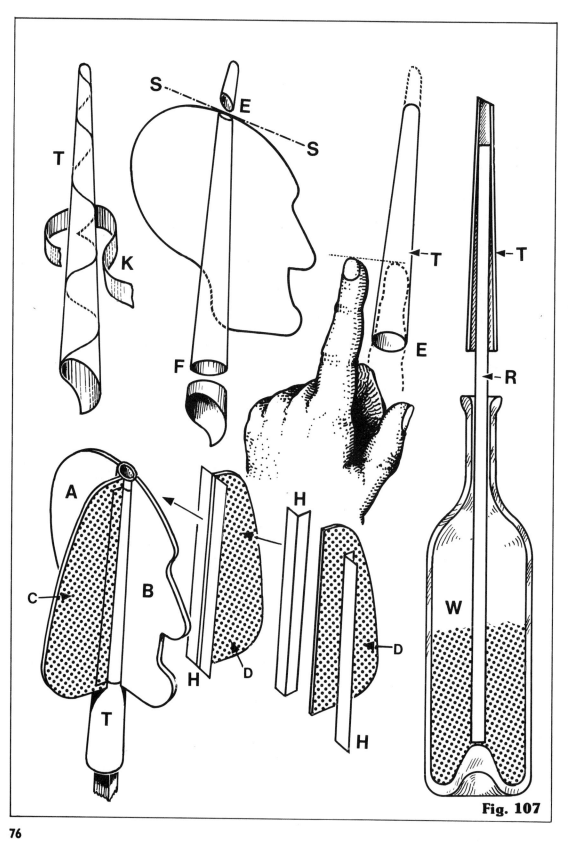

Fig. 107

The idea is to connect the four vertical pieces A, B, C and D, using horizontal or oblique levels whose placement you should mark on your pattern with dotted lines.

Fig. 108 shows the placement of one of these cross-levels M. Using pieces of gummed kraft paper, attach various cardboard levels like M around the tube T. After glueing each level, draw on it shape K of the head as shown, then cut the cardboard along line K. Note that you must also cut the innermost corner of M, shown at L, to leave a place for tube T to pass through the head.

The upper right-hand corner drawing in Fig. 108 shows the completed cardboard armature. Note that levels U and X are not horizontal, but pass through points that determine the width of the head. The most important aspect of this project is to determine at which points these supports are the most necessary.

Now you must make the cover—that is, the outer shell—for your armature. Keep in mind that no matter how large you make a head with this technique, because the entire inside is hollow, the head will be extremely lightweight.

Begin by cutting a good supply of gummed 1-inch- (25-mm-) wide kraft paper into lengthwise strips about ½ inch (12.5 cm) wide. You can cut these pieces quickly; they do not have to be exact.

Now cover the cardboard cross sections of the armature with these pieces of tape P. Hold them in place, as shown in Fig. 108, with strips of the same gummed tape Q. Attach all of the P strips together at the top of the head N. To do this, make a cross from two pieces of the gummed tape. The close-up in the middle of Fig. 108 shows cardboard section C with an attachment Q simply pinched in place around tape P.

When you have trimmed all of the cardboard edges in this fashion, attach additional strips between those already placed. These serve to outline the rest of the surface width of your head; see the drawing in the bottom right-hand corner of Fig. 108.

To avoid unnecessarily weighing down the head, you do not have to cover the entire surface with these strips. It is sufficient to form a sort of cage or lattice before you enclose the shape within a paper covering. When you are satisfied with the contour you have created, cover the armature with pieces of newpaper that have been soaked in glue. Add three or four coats in this manner. Be sure to smooth each coat carefully, and let it dry thoroughly before you add another.

When the last coat is completely dry, sand it lightly with fine sandpaper to remove any last folds or bumps in the surface. Cover the head with a coat of matt paint and decorate your creation with water-base paints or glued-on scraps of felt.

Finishing this project consists of adding the features not included in the base piece. For the head shown in Fig. 108, you must now add ears. Sometimes you might also need to add the eyes at the last moment. Then, you must also add some hair, which you can make from any material you wish: raffia, scraps of wool or cotton, strips of cloth or felt, for example.

Remember that such heads are so light that you can make them fairly large. In most instances, a classical costume which depends on being spread out by a puppeteer's fingers is inappropriate for this puppet. A costume that requires either only one hand or no hand at all is more desirable.

A typical example of this type of puppet is completely decorated with strips of felt rolled into curls. The use of hair or fur has been completely avoided, because they detract from the personality of the character. The eyes are made from large, fancy and imaginative-looking buttons.

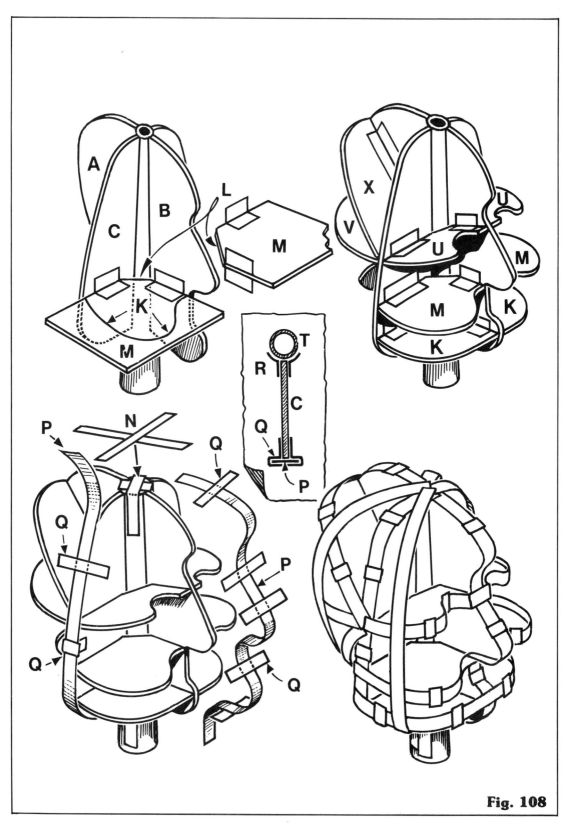

Fig. 108

Making the Costume

Clothing your puppet is just as important as making the puppet itself. We will not consider the very classical costumes be-cause they are too complicated for the puppets you have made. Instead, you will construct more practical, but no less imaginative, outfits.

Hand puppets like those you have been making lend themselves well to a lively stage show—they are not stiff, and they act naturally, thanks to their hands, which, of course, are animated by real human hands. In the past, puppets only had artificial hands, which hung limply at their sides.

Fig. 109 shows a puppet's head T. To construct the body, attach this head to a

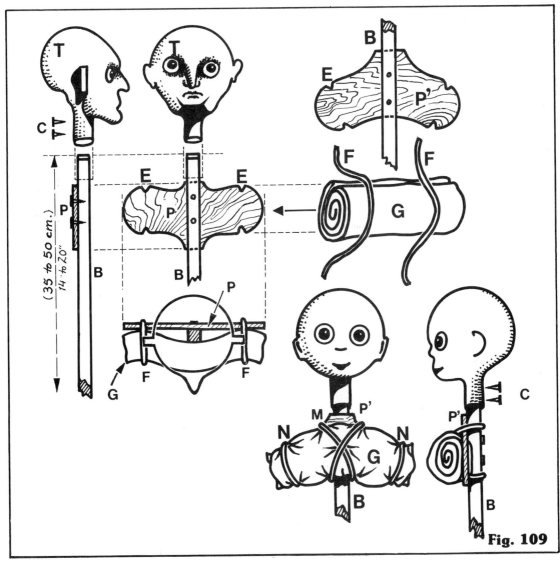

Fig. 109

stick B, which can be either squared or rounded. If the stick is squared, however, you can feel with your hands in which direction the head is facing as you manipulate the puppet. Use two large-headed nails to secure the head in place, as shown. Sometimes, you might prefer to nail the head to the body after you have completed the body and the costume. Keep in mind that the sleeve covering the body of the puppet—which is actually the puppet's skin—is different than the clothes with which you then dress your character.

The armature

To begin the body of your puppet, cut out a sort of "coat stand" P from plywood. Attach this piece behind stick B to form the line of the shoulders (see Fig. 109). Before you attach the shoulder piece P to the stick, however, notch it in the four places E shown in the drawing. Use these notches to attach a padding made from rolled-up rags or pieces of felt G, using pieces of string F. The bulk you create in this manner gives your puppet a chest. Be careful that the width and bulk of the chest you add are proportionate to the dimensions of the head.

Fig. 109 shows how to mount P behind B and G in front of P.

To make a female puppet, you should shape the armature as shown in P′, in which the shoulders are more sloped, to reduce the breadth of the shoulders. Also, you should attach P′ in front of B instead of behind it. Next, you need to add the padding. Notice in M in Fig. 109 that the end ties N cross in the middle of the front.

If your puppet is a dancer, you might also want to add a second level of padding that is lower than the first and in back of B which will serve as the hips. Make this padding in the same way you made the first one G.

The cloak

Choose some lining material that is inexpensive, not shiny and of a neutral color that's similar to the background paint of the head. Try to use a fabric that is about one yard (one metre) wide.

To make the cloak, you should cut a piece of the fabric that is 2L long—that is, equal to twice the width of the fabric L (see Fig. 110). Fold this length of material along line ab, as shown in Fig. 111. Sew from a to c, then from d to e. At a, leave a small opening through which you can pass the neck of the armature you have already made. Make a small stitch at f on each shoulder to attach the cloak to the padding G and to prevent the armature from moving (see Fig. 111).

When you sew the edges, leave a space about 3½ to 4 in. (9 to 10 cm) wide between c and d. You will sew the hand M to this opening. Unless you (or whoever is to be the puppeteer) are left-handed, this space is for your right hand. Otherwise, reverse the directions thus far given so you leave this opening on the other side of the fabric.

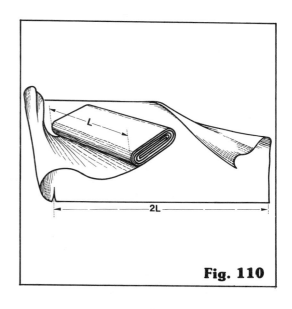

Fig. 110

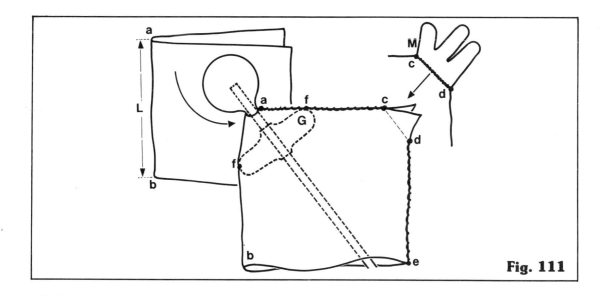

Fig. 111

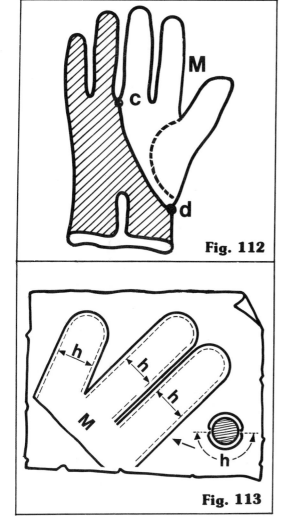

Fig. 112

Fig. 113

There are several different methods you can use to make the hand M. The easiest is shown in Fig. 112. Simply cut off from *c* to *d* on an old or mismatched glove, keeping only the thumb, index finger and middle finger. Instead, you can knit a thumb and two fingers to size—that is, to exactly fit your hand. This method allows the hand much flexibility. A third technique you could use is to make a glove from two identical pieces of felt, one for the back and one for the palm of the hand. Make a pattern of very large half-fingers. Measurement *h* in Fig. 113 should correspond to half the circumference of your fingers. Be sure to cut extra fabric all the way around to allow for sewing the two pieces together.

When you have finished making the hand, no matter which method you use, sew it between *c* and *d* in the corner of the cloak, to the right of the puppet-to-be, with the thumb on top.

Fig. 114 shows how you should hold your puppet by B in your left hand while your right hand, with two fingers folded back towards the inside of the cloak, propels the hand of the doll.

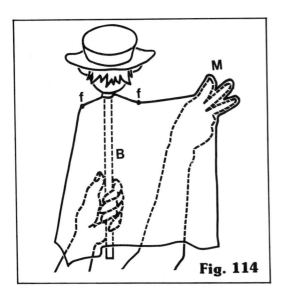

Fig. 114

How to dress up the sleeve puppet

Cape

A cape that simply covers the shoulders is shown in Fig. 115. You can cut a collar in any shape, such as N. You might find it necessary to attach the cape to the sleeve with small hidden stitches here and there so that the puppet's movements do not disturb its placement too much.

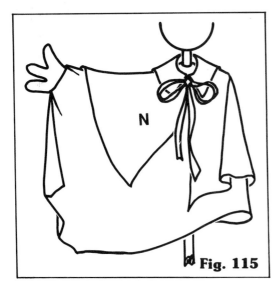

Fig. 115

Fig. 116

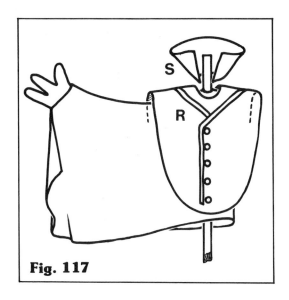

Fig. 117

Fig. 118

Breastplate

The breastplate looks like a sleeveless cloak R, as shown in Fig. 117, with or without a collar S. The breastplate, like the cape, is an elegant device for avoiding the problem of the right sleeve, which is difficult to do, and is discussed in more detail later.

Simple covering

The covering shown in Fig. 118 is composed of a rectangle of cloth or felt U. You make a series of slits in this piece through which you pass a piece of ribbon. When you tighten the ribbon around the neck, you form creases and folds, as shown.

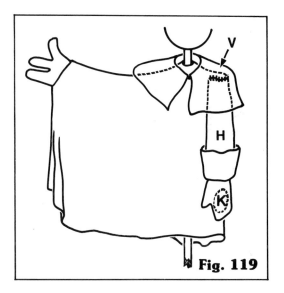

Fig. 119

False arms

For certain characters, and to create visual symmetry, you might wish to portray not only the moveable right arm, but also the stationary left arm.

Fig. 119 shows you how to sew on a sleeve H, elongated by a felt hand, which is a kind of mitten weighted down from the inside with a stone or other heavy object K. Notice in Fig. 119 that the stitching on the top, which attaches the sleeve to the cloak, is concealed under a fairly large collar V.

Following are some examples of different characters you can create with costumes.

A Constable

Fig. 121

Fig. 120 shows how you can solve the problem of the right sleeve (which must allow your arm to easily pass through to manoeuvre the puppet). You cannot use a normal sleeve to do this (see Fig. 114).

To do this for a constable, cut a piece of felt W, which you elongate with the wrist covering X of a white glove (see Fig. 123). Glue or sew on the straps, buttons and medals, as shown. Make the epaulet Z by glueing fringed pieces of felt to a cardboard base underneath. Note that the left epaulet hides the attachment of the false sleeve Y.

Make the cap separately from the head so you can remove it whenever you like. Measure around the head and shape a piece of cardboard so that the hat fits exactly. Cover the cardboard with felt.

Fig. 122

Fig. 120

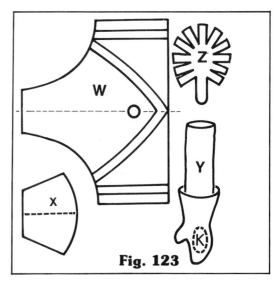

Fig. 123

A Country Boy

Fig. 124 illustrates that it is possible for your puppet to have a pair of legs. This can be particularly useful if you want to make a dancer who can perform on stage or a narrator who can sit jauntily on the edge of the stage.

Notice in Fig. 125 that to form the legs, you must make a wooden armature J going from the feet to the knees. Cover the foot with leather or felt in any shape you wish. Make the legs of the trousers from a sleeve of fabric D. Hang the armature J from the puppet at B, using a piece of ribbon or string. You must, of course, hide this suspension with a jacket or other article of clothing. Also be sure to conceal the sewing at the top part of D with this covering.

Fig. 125 clearly shows how you should hide your arm inside the cloak, which you should make as neutral a color as possible.

Fig. 124

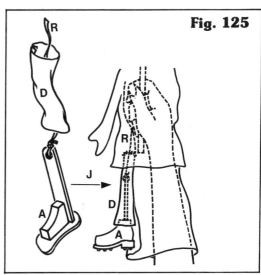

Fig. 125

Animal Puppets

show. Shape lightweight cardboard or heavyweight paper cones around these discs to form the head and body. Paint them grey or cover them with grey felt.

Next cut out two cardboard ears shaped like E, and cover them with grey felt. Nail them to each side of the head. Finish by adding the eyes, whiskers and tail as pictured.

Chicks

You can easily make a whole family of chicks and other winged creatures, which you hold and manoeuvre with a single stick. There are many different ways in which you can create these animals, and the suggestions here should only serve to direct you along a creative path.

Fig. 127 shows a rooster in the process of being created. Notice that the stick M supports a rectangular piece of wood E for the beak. Screw or nail E to M. Glue wooden discs such as Y on either side of this construction to form the head. Then screw or nail on another wooden disc D which is larger and thicker than the first two. To this, attach an armature C for the body. Then make a kind of sack S from felt to fit over armature C. Stuff this sack with rags or wood shavings, and nail it onto D.

Make one or more round, curved tails R from strands of rattan. Insert these tails into the stuffed sack. Fig. 127 shows how you transform each such strand of rattan into a plume of feathers by glueing multicolored pieces of felt over them.

Fig. 128 shows the finished rooster. Notice that the body is covered with strips of felt X, which form feathers. You can create an especially exciting puppet if you use real feathers rather than felt ones. Glue one or more pieces shaped like H to the front of the body. Then cut pieces G and K to fit the head and the neck, as shown in the drawing.

Now, you might be interested in making some animal puppets for your little theatre.

Mouse

Besides birds, there are several other types of animal puppets you can make to mount on a single stick. See, for example, the mouse in Fig. 126. To make this mouse, nail two discs D, one for the head and one for the body, to the stick M. Naturally, this stick remains well hidden behind the stage of your theatre during a

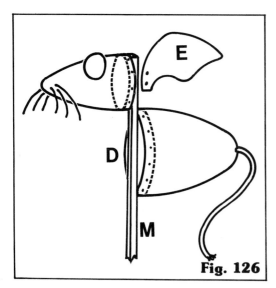

Fig. 126

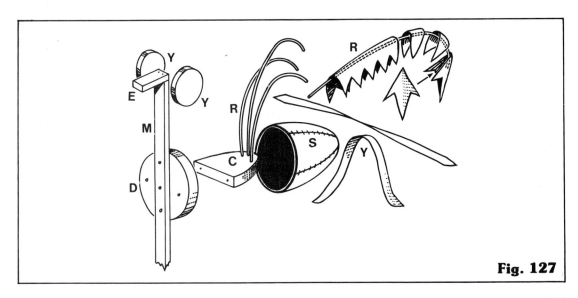

Fig. 127

Fig. 128

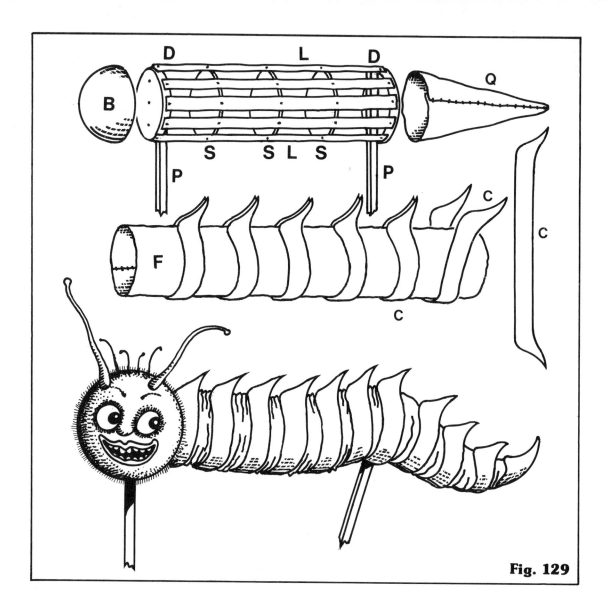

Fig. 129

Caterpillar

Although the two preceding types of animals are built round a single stick, most animal puppets are equipped with two sticks (one in front, one in back), and must be manipulated with two hands. Using two hands is more difficult than using only one,

but you can produce marvelous movements in this way—for example, the swish of a tail, the turning of a head, and so on.

The caterpillar pictured in Fig. 129 is one example of a two-sectioned puppet. You can make the caterpillar as long as you want. Fig. 129 shows one way to proceed. Make two discs of wood D and attach them to the ends of two sticks P. Join the two discs with strips of elastic L, whose shape you can maintain by inserting several lightweight plywood discs, S, S and S. Cover the head end with half of a children's rubber ball B. On the other end of the animal, add a felt tail Q, which you should stuff slightly; nail round D.

Next make the covering F long enough to stretch thoroughly along the whole length of the caterpillar. Decorate F by glueing to it strips of green felt shaped like C. Because this glued-on felt is fairly stiff, be sure you use a very flexible fabric for the covering underneath. When the caterpillar rests, this fabric looks accordion-pleated. Decorate the head as you wish.

You must be careful to manoeuvre the caterpillar in such a way that the two support sticks are level with the edge of the stage, so they are invisible to the audience.

Hobby horse

This is a high-ranking member of the family of toy animals. Fig. 130 shows one way in which you can create this important creature. Attach a bedspring Z between

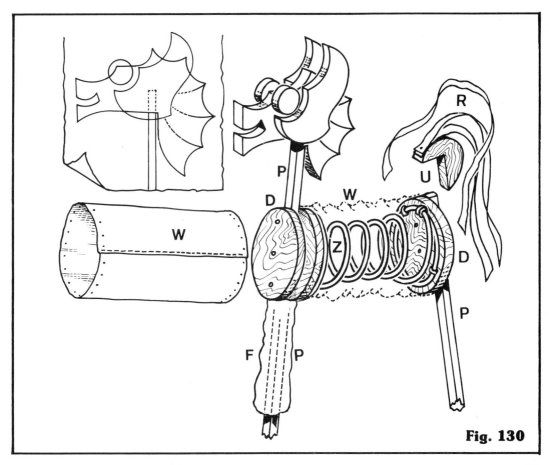

Fig. 130

Fig. 131

two wooden discs D, using several two-pointed nails. Then sew together a sleeve W from felt and nail it securely to D.

You can make the head from cardboard, wood or padded rags—whichever you wish. The head in Fig. 130 is made of wood cut out according to the pattern shown. Felt was glued to the head to decorate it.

To make a tail like the one shown, cut out a small square of wood U and notch it as shown. Attach a cluster of felt ribbons R to this piece.

Finally, you can add coverings like F to clothe the paws and the neck.

Fig. 132

Cow

Using the same principle of a bedspring body, you can make a wonderful cow like the one shown in Fig. 131. Make the head from a disc of wood D to which you attach cutout wooden ears H. Nail the horns G to the head, as shown.

Now take half of an appropriately sized child's rubber ball B. Carefully sew two pieces of cardboard tubing T to it. Cover the front of these tubes with a muzzle M, which you cut out from plywood.

Notch B for the ears as shown in the drawing and fit round D. Nail everything in place. To finish, add eyes C. You can make the eyes from table-tennis balls, bottle caps, big bright buttons or anything else you like.

Of course, you should cover this armature with felt. Add a tail, which you make from a piece of cord and a bunch of flowing ribbons you tie to the cord.

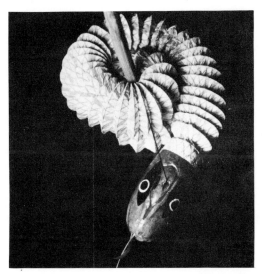

Fig. 133

Making a Puppet Theatre

No matter what type of puppet theatre you construct, you must be sure it meets three basic requirements: (1) it must hide the puppeteers; (2) it must have a large enough opening for the acting to take place and this opening must have a shelf B ("the strip") along which the puppets can move; and (3) it must provide sufficient lighting for the dolls.

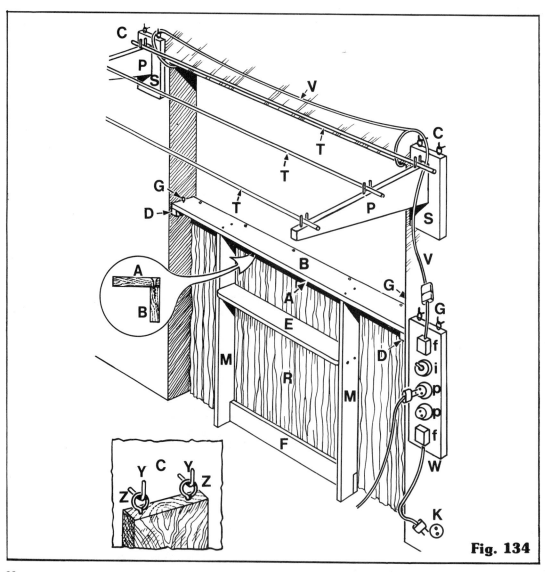

Fig. 134

The puppet theatre presented here is simple to make right in a wide doorway that is either bordered with two folding or swinging doors or is simply a single opening (see Fig. 134).

To begin, you make a frame from wooden boards M, M, E and F. This frame supports strip A-B, which is assembled at right angles, as shown in the drawing. The ends of B rest on two brackets attached to the wall (D, D). Thread two bolts (G, G) through two holes in the ends of B to stabilize the entire construction. Nail a curtain made from a type of opaque fabric along A. Notice that the puppeteers can place certain props on shelf E during the show. The spaces between M and the wall can be used by the puppeteers to pass from the wings into the room.

You can hang additional curtains—changes of scenery, decorations or backgrounds—from metal curtain rods or

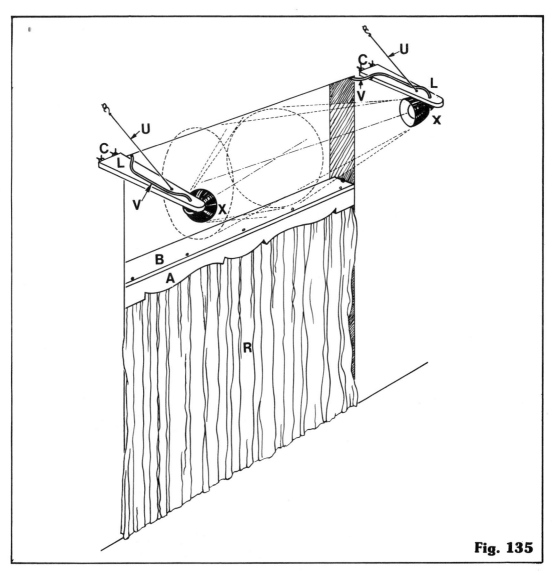

Fig. 135

tubes T, T and T. You place each of these rods between a pair of nails hammered into two crossbeams P and P, which are attached to the foundations S and S as shown. Hang this S and P arrangement by a simple system C which you compose from two screw-rings Z and two L-shaped hooks Y, shown in the inset in Fig. 134.

To remove the theatre from the doorway, unhook C and remove the G bolts.

The electrical device for this theatre is entirely contained on a wooden board W which you also hang from the wall using the C system of screw rings and L-shaped hooks. You will need an outlet K near the doorway to provide the electrical current for the spotlights. The current should pass from K through a fuse f, and then supply the circuit breaker i of the spotlights for the stage and the two outlets p and p for any additional lights, bells or record players.

You can direct the current towards the spotlights by a cable V which you hang above the stage. Notice in Fig. 134 that this cable V has two segments—one to the right and one to the left of the stage.

Fig. 135 shows the audience side of this puppet theatre. Notice the position of the two spotlights X and X above and about one yard (one metre) in front of the stage. This placement ensures that their lights cross on the opening. You can either just place these spotlights or you can hang them on arms such as L and L, which you can attach to the wall from L-shaped hooks like the ones you used to make C. Notice in Fig. 135 that two cables U and U, hung from screw rings, maintain these L arms level. An electrical wire V comes from the wings as previously described. Connect these to high-powered lightbulbs.

You can construct a puppet theatre such as the one just described with hardly any tools. After you disassemble such a theatre, all that remains are several L-shaped hooks in the wall and several brackets D screwed into the doorway.

A Transportable Puppet Theatre

If you do not have a convenient doorway available, you can easily construct a detachable one.

Fig. 136 shows that this transportable theatre consists of a wooden frame that you can either make yourself or have a carpenter build for you. It consists of three wooden frames assembled with hinges somewhat like a folding screen. Preferably, the central panel should be double the width of either of the two side panels, so that you can fold back the side sections behind the middle one to put away the theatre when you are finished with it.

Nail or screw on two squared bars of wood J and J to the top outside edge of the side panels. To these pieces of wood, you should then attach two more strips of wood U and U, which hold the spotlights X and X at their ends. Use bolts and wing nuts as shown at H in Fig. 136 to attach U. This allows you to easily unscrew the pieces to dismantle the theatre. This assembly is shown in detail in the left-hand, circled close-up in Fig. 136.

The second circled close-up in Fig. 136 shows how you should construct strip B so that it, too, is detachable. Nail two parallel planks underneath B to form a groove, into which you insert the edge of the stage.

Decorate the panel openings of the screen with some type of opaque fabric. If you prefer, you can fill in these areas with pieces of plywood instead.

Next, you can screw the electrical plate W in place where shown in Fig. 136. This piece is also easy to detach when you dismantle the theatre. The electricity comes

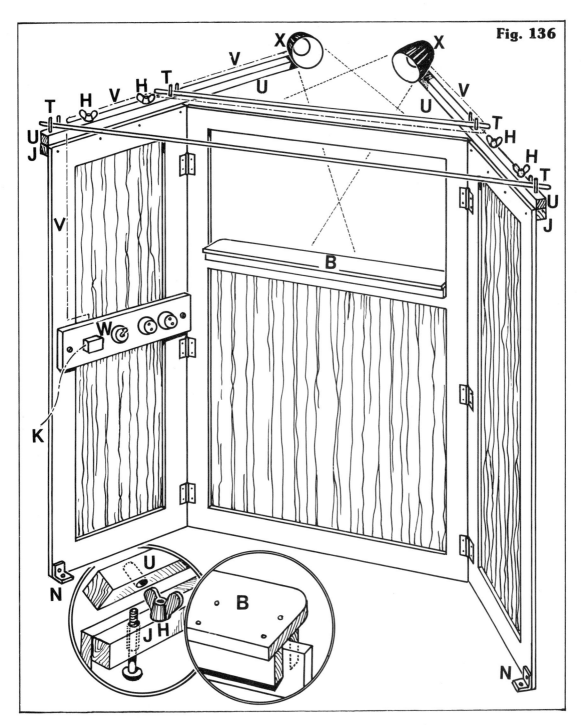

from K. The dotted-and-dashed line in Fig. 136 shows the path of a plastic-coated electrical wire from the circuit breaker W to the two spotlights X and X.

Notice, finally, the two small squares of metal N and N, which are screwed to the bottom of the two side panels of the theatre. If you usually set up this theatre in the same location, you can turn two small screws right into two small holes in the floor to attach the theatre to the spot, which greatly enhances the stability of the theatre.

Index